Learning at an Early Age

A CURRICULUM FOR YOUNG CHILDREN

Learning at an Early Age

A CURRICULUM FOR YOUNG CHILDREN

VOLUME 2

Helen F. Robison and
Sydney L. Schwartz

Prentice-Hall, Inc., Englewood Cliffs, New Jersey

To Kenneth D. Wann

© 1972

by PRENTICE-HALL, Inc.,
Englewood Cliffs, New Jersey

Printed in the United States of America

ISBN: 0-13-527598-9

10 9 8 7 6 5 4 3 2 1

PRENTICE-HALL INTERNATIONAL, INC., *London*
PRENTICE-HALL OF AUSTRALIA, PTY. LTD., *Sydney*
PRENTICE-HALL OF CANADA, LTD., *Toronto*
PRENTICE-HALL OF INDIA PRIVATE LIMITED, *New Delhi*
PRENTICE-HALL OF JAPAN, INC., *Tokyo*

Acknowledgments

We are grateful to the many persons who contributed to the development of this curriculum for children. Of the many school administrators, supervisors, teachers, and teacher aides with whom we worked, we would like to mention especially New York City teachers Martha Sellers, Chelley Gutin, and Harriet Dorosin.

Students and collaborators who made unique contributions to the program included David Wickens, Maureen Herman, Sylvia Ross, and Irene Slaymaker.

Finally, to our families, who were patient, understanding, and helpful throughout the years from the original idea to the completion of this book, our heartfelt thanks.

Contents

INTRODUCTION   1

COGNITIVE SKILLS   9

MUSIC STRUCTURE MODELS   27

LANGUAGE   53

MATHEMATICS   93

SCIENCE   145

SOCIOLOGY   165

GEOGRAPHY   193

ECONOMICS   207

APPENDIX
    Child Behavior Test (CBT)   220
    Recommended Program Sequence: First Month   227
    Teaching Plans: First Month   228
    Recommended Changes in Program Sequence
    for Second Month of Program   231
    Sample Weekly Teaching Plan   233
    Activities Analysis Form (AAF)   235
    Child Progress Forms   240

Introduction

Learning At An Early Age: A Curriculum for Young Children is a revised version of an experimental program developed in concert with classroom teachers of four- and five-year-old children in the inner city of New York. This volume, together with Vol. I, *Learning at an Early Age: A Programmed Text for Teachers*, provides a preservice and inservice guide for the implementation of a comprehensive prekindergarten and kindergarten curriculum. This curriculum features intellectual stimulation and language development and is based on continuous assessment of teaching procedures, children's learning, and teaching-learning interactions.

This curriculum emphasizes individual pacing, each child's uniqueness, and a wide range of teacher roles and strategies, which help to stabilize and increase children's intellectual and linguistic development. Affective development is charted through acceptance of children's feelings, positive channeling of aggression, and fostering autonomy in many specific ways. Feelings of competence through mastery of various tasks and the development of family approval of the child's achievements in visible skills areas, are the main sources of motivation.

Learning activities, in this curriculum, flow from spontaneous, self-chosen play situations, to specific structured tasks, games, and constructional projects. Informality and individual choices within well-defined limits prevail throughout the program. Individual or tutorial instruction is stressed, with considerable de-emphasis of total group activities. Social development is emphasized through procedures of classroom management, encouragement of independence and self-regulation, and teacher guidance in conflict situations.

Cognitive and language development are specifically programmed through playful experiences, and through sequenced, detailed and structured tasks, games, and teacher-child and child-child interactions.

This curriculum draws mainly on elements from child development theory, empirical studies of young children's classroom learning, linguistic theory, curriculum developments in specific content areas, and diagnosed learning needs of individual children. Such developmental theorists as Jean Piaget and O. K. Moore are especially drawn upon, in their emphases upon play and natural development, but the program seeks to stabilize and increase the child's cognitive and linguistic growth through effective teacher roles in the classroom. Included in this curriculum is a total program comprising a detailed plan for teaching in seven program areas. The content areas are as follows: Cognitive Skills, Music, Language, Mathematics, Science, Sociology, Geography, and Economics. Each of these content areas includes a set of structure models, or suggested teaching designs. The structure models, which are specific protocols for initiating and guiding instructional episodes, include a list of behavioral goals, materials required, teaching procedures, and suggestions for variations of materials and activities. As the teacher comes to know the goals and procedures of this curriculum, it will seem quite natural for her to substitute her own ideas for the educative activities suggested in the protocols. Teachers are expected to select additional activities from their own repertoire to multiply opportunities for children to practice the selected learnings. Gradually, each teacher will invest her own individual creativity in teaching sequences to replace these samples of teaching. Thus, while the curriculum design may have the appearance of being totally prescriptive, it is not intended to restrict or confine the teacher from improvising alternate activities for the same purposes.

Parents are expected to become involved in the program in as many ways as possible. They may be classroom volunteers, paid paraprofessionals, visitors, consultants, resource persons, especially talented in various ways, or sources of ideas, materials, or feedback on children's learning. In some instances, parents may wish to develop related workshops to coordinate home and school learning, to set up and operate a lending library of materials or equipment, or to develop their own ideas in other ways.

Many of the suggested activities in this curriculum are familiar to experienced teachers of young children. However, what is new is the detailed organization of learning activities in specific relationship to learning goals and the sequencing and coordination of these learning goals and activities. Each structure model reinforces previous learning and builds upon this learning while introducing the new learning task. The learning goals are identical for all children. However, the rate of progress toward these goals is individual and unique for each child. The plan for teaching is based on a diagnosis of each child's learning ability, his skills and understandings, and his interest, so that the tutorials, which are one-to-one instructional episodes, and small group instructional activities with 2 to 5 children, may be initiated with specified learning goals identified. Knowledge of the unique interests of the participating child directs the selection of materials for use with that child. Continuous diagnosis of learning levels provides the information needed to select structure models that utilize the child's competency or skills as new learnings are initiated.

The teacher is expected to be sensitive to individual children's developmental and unique needs, and to be flexible in planning to meet these needs. Individualizing the curriculum includes the need to simplify or to introduce complexity as the situation warrants, and to let the child take the lead in demonstrating his preferences for materials, activities and play content.

The spontaneous play behavior of children offers the base for many teaching sequences, as well as providing needed diagnostic information and self-directed practice activities. This program is rooted in and takes shape only in a multi-activity classroom, most commonly found in programs for 4- and 5-year-olds, which allow children to decide what to play and for how long. As children have choices, so do the teachers. That is, while children are engaged in interest centers of their own choosing, the teacher may select the structure model or learning task matched to the learning level of the child or children with whom she plans to work. As the members of the group pursue their self-selected activities, the teacher may extend an invitation for participation and implement an activity.

The curriculum is based on a developmental view of the young child's progress in his interrelated physical, social, emotional, and cognitive growth. Four- and five-year-olds are expected to learn through intensive sensory-motor activity and the manipulation of things. They learn a great deal from each other. They also learn much from the language of the adults with whom they work, from the behavior of these adults and from the expectations of these adults. Further, this curriculum assumes that children are continuously learning, and the task of the school is to channel this learning energy toward increased competence in understandings and skills of interaction with the physical and social environment. For the young child, channeling his learning energy means pursuing new learning through activities that capture his interest and capitalize on what he already knows and can do. In this way, the child will tend to choose to undertake or repeat the learning many times, with or without the presence and active involvement of the adult. The child also draws other children into his learning activities, so that as one child masters new skills, his peers are exposed to his new interests and become involved in his playful use of these skills.

Volume 1 discusses in detail the assumptions implicit in this curriculum about children as learners, the organization and administration of the classroom learning environment, and strategies for teaching. These assumptions, while not specifically stated in the structure models are clearly a part of the program, and include the following:

1. Teacher expectations for children's activity and progress are conveyed through the clarity, selectivity, and attractiveness of the arrangement of materials and equipment. For example, Chapter 3, "The Physical Environment," discusses many aspects of organizing, equipping, and maintaining classroom materials and interest centers for learning.

2. Rules and procedures for classroom management facilitate children's growth toward independence. See Vol. 1, Chapter 4, "Classroom Management," for a comprehensive discussion of features of classroom management

which foster social learning in the classroom.

3. Teacher relationships with children are established on a one-to-one basis, valuing individual differences in interests, maturation, and life experiences. See Vol. 1, Chapter 5, "Learning Activities," for discussion of types of learning activities provided to meet individual differences.

4. Social-emotional and physical learnings, which constitute a major goal of prekindergarten and kindergarten programs, can be developed comfortably within the context of meaningful activities. Therefore, this curriculum design coordinates social-emotional and physical learnings within specific activities in content areas or as a part of the routines of daily repetitive features of classroom life. In Vol. 1, Chapter 7, "Program Goals," and Chapter 4, "Classroom Management," offer elaboration of goals and ways to feature the desired learnings in routines and in instructional activities.

5. Though teaching styles are expected to be unique for each teacher, teaching procedures have some common features, such as:

a. Questioning children follows rather than precedes teaching sequences.

b. Testing for diagnostic purposes to guide teaching decisions is completed as a distinct and separate episode from an instructional episode.

c. Demonstration is offered simultaneously with verbalization, whenever possible, until there is clear evidence that verbalization alone is understood.

d. Labeling and descriptive language are used freely in natural situations, with the offer of new vocabulary in context of action and manipulation.

e. Problem-solving tasks are proposed only when children have learned the skills needed to solve them and are likely to be successful.

f. Teaching plans are differentiated for individual children, so that as each child reaches stable mastery of a task, he is offered a more complex task. Or if a child needs simpler tasks, teaching sequences are shifted to help him reach a level of success. For a detailed discussion of teacher roles and strategies, see Vol. 1, Chapter 4, "The Human Environment, Teacher Roles and Strategies."

6. Language development, which is critical to expanding learning for young children, is maximized when children produce speech spontaneously and extensively as they engage in activities and conversations with their peers and teachers. Language learning is fostered as teachers elaborate and expand children's utterances appropriately and in context, as suggested in many of the structure models. This curriculum design assumes that children's speech

learning depends to a great extent on their spontaneous generation of the speech forms they hear within the context of activities of genuine interest. That is, where the speech forms children hear give increased meaning to the activity in progress, or offer verbalization about what they are doing, want to do, or have done, teachers are encouraged to feature such verbal interaction.

Since everyone speaks a "dialect," all dialects are valued equally. Since it is desirable for the children to acquire the school dialect in addition to their home dialect, the goal becomes dialectal flexibility, where the children may use either dialect comfortably and appropriately, as they develop the ability to distinguish the dialect which is relevant to a given situation. Correction of children's speech inhibits language learning, while an environment that stimulates language production fosters language learning. See Vol. 1, Chapter 7, "Program Goals, Language and Cognitive Goals," for extensive discussion of this aspect.

In addition to the implicit assumptions listed previously, there are some explicit features of this curriculum which may be summarized as follows:

1. While the classroom program for children reflects flexibility, freedom of choice, and movement, and diversity of activities, the framework for this pattern is precise planning, with clear identification by the teacher of selected goals for each child, based on his development and his pattern of interest in activity involvement. This means that record-keeping is essential to the teaching procedure. Sample forms for keeping records which have developed in cooperation with teachers who have worked with this curriculum are found on pages 240 to 247. The purpose of these forms is to substitute records for memory about children's progress, and to make available to all members of the teaching team the important information on each child. These records show what a child has mastered, what he is working on now, and his current interests. For detailed discussion of recording children's progress, see Vol. 1, Chapter 8, "Evaluation." It is expected that each teacher will select or devise her own procedures for record-keeping.

2. A broad-based diagnostic assessment, the Child Behavior Test (CBT), which crosses most of the content areas in this curriculum, is suggested to obtain a profile on each child (see pages 220 to 227). This diagnostic form may be administered in the fall and again in the spring, or partitioned into sections for administration at various times during the year. A profile, such as this one, which is directly related to the behavioral goals as stated in the curriculum, aids in planning for children's learning activities. See Vol. 1, Chapter 8, for further suggestions for evaluation of children's progress.

3. All activities provided within the program may contribute to children's progress toward the program goals. Many activities are pursued by

the children after introduction by the teacher, and many activities are developed by the teacher after children explore the use of materials on their own. Teacher involvement with children's learning may take the form of leading the willing child into a task, cooperating with the child who is already pursuing a task, or enriching the child's activity as he directs its development.

4. Instructional moves by the teacher are sequenced to lead to the learning goals. Therefore, the effectiveness of teaching behavior may be assessed by comparing children's achievement with the behavioral goals.

5. Teaching strategies follow a consistent sequence in all structure models, as follows:

a. Offer of choices in play with selected materials for self-directed play or a task.

b. Child manipulation of materials as a first step to the development of the play or task.

c. Introduction of structure for play with materials features a series of inputs by the teacher with children contributing and responding spontaneously as they perceive the task. These inputs generally follow a fixed sequence:

(1) Introduction of verbal labels of materials and actions as both teacher and child manipulate materials.

(2) Specification of a task. Find the child's level of competence in a task by suggesting performance of a behavior of which the child has been observed to be capable.

(3) Transformation of a task, if necessary, to a simpler or more complex level, observing the child's performance with the materials.

(4) As the task is achieved, vary it slightly by changing the materials or leaving several children to pursue the task together as self-directed group activity.

6. Most of the curriculum content is interdependent and overlapping, as indicated by the extensive cross-referencing across the various content areas. This makes it possible for teachers to identify multiple learning goals for each activity.

7. Only when children take over the learning activity and practice on their own, is it clear that they are stabilizing the desired learning. As children indicate readiness to take over or direct the learning activity, they are encouraged to do so. Rapid learners are often helped to reinforce their learning by working with children who express a desire for guided practice in a task.

8. Children learn in a variety of participation patterns, active or passive, and are encouraged to continue to learn in diverse ways. These include observation of other children's work, peripheral participation, or active central or leading patterns. Note that many of the structure models explicitly state, "Others may watch."

9. Children become competent by using newly acquired skills in many different settings and finding many reasons to use them. Some children practice new skills spontaneously, while other children need teacher-planned opportunities for practice.

10. There is a clear distinction between teaching and testing, which are two quite different teaching behaviors and require distinctive implementation. That is, instructional episodes do not include testing procedures, and testing or diagnostic episodes usually exclude instructional components. Teaching episodes are designed so that children will experience success, whereas testing is designed to find out the limits of what children know and can do. To find limits requires overshooting them and identifying the levels at which children fail.

Implementation of the *Curriculum for Young Children* requires consideration of the following elements of early childhood classrooms, which are discussed at length in Vol. 1:

1. The arrangement of the physical environment based on interest centers where children choose to engage in learning activities and acquire increasing independence in pursuing their interests.

2. The scheduling of the program to minimize the time required for transitions and management routines, in order to maximize the teacher's instructional time and children's involvement in the program. See pages 227 to 230 for a suggested program schedule for the first month of the year, for the regular schedule.

3. Preplanning for sequencing introduction of structure models in the seven content areas. Suggested order considering both parallel learning goals and sequential learning goals are provided for each content area.

4. Establishment of procedures for (a) diagnostic activities, which precede instructional planning for each child, and (b) maintenance of progress records for each child, noting which structure models have been mastered, or are in process, as well as learning goals currently pursued. See suggestions for recording forms, on page 240 to 247.

5. Evaluation of teaching strategies, at regular intervals. One form developed by the authors which offers a structure for analyzing teaching behavior in an early childhood classroom is the Activities Analysis Form

(AAF), which appears on pages 235 to 240, with instructions for its use. Teachers who have used this form report that it helped in objectifying and analyzing features of their teaching behavior in a way that allowed them to try out modifications. This form requires practice in use, with one professional observing another in a cooperative team format, or alone, using the videotape recorder for later replay, to code and study teaching behavior. Instructions for use of this form should be studied carefully before coding samples of teaching behavior. It should be noted that, as with any instrument for coding teaching behavior, practice is required to reach reliability.

6. Cooperative teaching with the procedures for involvement of all adults in the setting, each assuming mutually agreed upon responsibilities for guiding learning activities. This requires planning time for evaluation of program development and children's learning, and assignment of teaching tasks for each day or week, as desired.

7. Packaging materials for tasks. Planning to implement structure models includes packaging alternate sets of materials to appeal to different children, and labeling and packaging these sets for efficient use. A list of suggested materials is found in Vol. 1, chapter 3. Included are recommended materials for early childhood classrooms, as well as materials needed to develop specified teaching sequences.

In the process of implementing a new curriculum, it is well to expect that time is needed to try out the new teaching models, and that retooling is a slow procedure requiring continuous assessment of the congruence of the classroom experience with the proposed model, as well as designing new models.

Cognitive Skills

2.00   Goals in Cognitive Skills
2.10   Manipulation of Objects
2.11   Same-Different Objects
2.12   Slap Down (Adaptation of Slap Jack)
2.13   Same-Different Pictures
2.20   Object Patterns
2.21   Chart: Summary of Patterning
2.22   Color Patterns
2.23   Copying Pattern Cards
2.24   Completing, Extending, and Creating Patterns
2.25   Transforming Color Patterns to Noncolor Designs
2.30   Sorting and Classifying

2.00 GOALS IN COGNITIVE SKILLS

There are several basic forms of cognitive activity which apply to all content areas. Important cognitive skills include comparison and contrast, patterning, classifying, and generalizing.

Four- and five-year-olds' thinking is based primarily upon their perceptions of the concrete, physical world as they interact with it. Beginning school experiences require the sensory-motor types of activities with which the child functions comfortably. The learning activities are planned so that the child begins to deal with pictures and words along with manipulation of concrete objects. Ultimately, the child's independence from the physical and concrete begins to grow as conceptual thinking develops.

Three factors govern the sequence and order of complexity of learning experiences:

1. *Repetition*: Repetition of experience is basic to young children's stable learning.
2. *Independence*: As needs for repetition decline, children's tasks can be increasingly independent, with less teacher assistance and with fewer cues.
3. *Abstraction*: As children's independence grows, their need for physical and concrete representations gradually decreases. Ultimately, children become capable of abstract thought.

Patterning is viewed as a basic cognitive skill which offers children practice in relating parts to the whole, in abstracting repeatable series in such forms as colors, numbers, shapes, letters of the alphabet, words and sentences, and in identifying arbitrary units. Patterning activities are featured in this area as well as in the mathematics, language, and science areas.

Behavioral Goals

1. Comparison and Contrast
   a. Children compare and contrast properties of concrete objects based on sensory perception.
   b. Children find *same* and *different* relationships of various physical attributes, actions, musical tones, rhythmic and melodic patterns, letters, numerals, and words.
2. Patterning
   a. Children identify and copy patterns by such properties as color, shape, size, rhythm, and tone.
   b. Children copy a pattern of concrete objects from a model.
   c. Children replicate and extend two-dimensional patterns, including pictures and color charts, with concrete objects.

    d.   Children replicate and extend a prescribed pattern with two-dimensional materials.

    e.   Children verbally identify a pattern and check it by reading it.

    f.   Children create patterns and label them.

3. Classifying
    a. Children experience extensive manipulation of objects so that they put like things together, based on physical properties.
    b. Children sort and classify objects based upon physical properties.
    c. Children sort objects into specified groups and label the groups.
    d. Children evidence understanding of grouping by completing a sorting of objects, based on physical properties.
    e. Children use different classifications for the same group of objects, beginning with physical properties and gradually changing to function and relationships.
    f. Children use two criteria simultaneously to sort a group of objects.

4. Generalizing
    a. Children observe simple rules required by games.
    b. Children devise simple rules required by games.
    c. Children predict a simple rule and test it.

Further Reference

    For teaching suggestions to foster the need to generalize, see especially:

Music 3.12, 3.30, 3.40-3.44
Language 4.12-4.19
Mathematics 5.31, 5.41, 5.42, 5.44, 5.50, 5.81
Science 6.20-6.22, 6.30, 6.40
Geography 8.20

2.10 MANIPULATION OF OBJECTS
GROUP SIZE: 1, 2, 5

Behavioral Goal

Children experience extensive manipulation of objects, so that they put like things together, based on physical properties.

Procedure

Materials

Select from all classroom content areas. Include:

Blocks	Craft materials
Block accessories	Science materials
Manipulation games	Math materials
Construction games	Woodworking materials
Art materials	Housekeeping equipment
Waterplay materials	Other classroom materials

1. Invite children to manipulate classroom materials playfully.
2. Encourage children to experience the full range of classroom materials.
3. When children tend to limit themselves to the same type of manipulation of the same materials, make suggestions for changes in handling, or invite children to work with some different attractive materials.
4. Help children explore properties of objects by action, manipulation, and experimentation.
5. Use clean-up time to begin sorting things that go together. See Cog. Skills 2.30 for further details.
6. Offer children muffin tins or egg boxes to sort out small objects at clean-up time. Give the children plenty of time to sort the objects.
7. Let children determine how to sort objects into muffin tins or egg boxes. If they are unable to make any decisions for sorting, make a suggestion.

Further Reference

Cognitive Skills 2.30

2.11 SAME-DIFFERENT OBJECTS
GROUP SIZE: 1, 2, 5

Behavioral Goals

1. Children label two objects as the same or not the same, or different.
2. Children select two objects and label them as the same or not the same.

Procedure

Materials

Select 8 pairs of identical objects from the following:

2 red marbles

2 miniature hammers

2 red fire engines

2 miniature chairs

Sheets of 8½ x 11 inch construction paper, 1 for each participant

Loop

1. Diagnostic check. Prepare a loop with a random assortment of some materials listed above. Give child remainder of these materials and ask him to find objects the same as each one and to arrange them in pairs. Skip steps 2 through 6 for those children who show mastery of this skill.
2. Invite children to look at collection of miniature objects, and allow time for free manipulation.
3. Begin game by holding up one object at a time and labeling it. "This is a fire engine. This is another fire engine. These two are the same."
4. After labeling all objects, place one object on each child's paper and ask him to find one that is the *same*.
5. Help child check selection. If child's selection is correct, say "This one is a red fire engine and this one is a red fire engine. They are the same." If child's selection is incorrect, say "This one is a red fire engine and this one is a chair. They are not the same. Find a red fire engine like this."
6. Repeat steps 3 through 5 until child is able to perform task with the initial collection.

Variations

1. Set up objects in pairs, some matched and some unmatched. Ask one child to find all pairs that are the *same*, and another child to find objects that are *not the same or different*.

2. Ask children to *stand up* when you hold up two objects that are the *same* and to *sit down* when you hold two objects that are *different*.

2.12 SLAP DOWN (ADAPTATION OF SLAP JACK)
GROUP SIZE: 2, 5

Behavioral Goals

1. Children match picture to object, labeling them as the same.
2. Children match picture to picture, labeling them as the same.

Procedure

Materials

Deck of 25 picture cards, with 5 pictures of each object. Five objects that match picture cards.

1. Help children label objects, then pictures.
2. Deal cards face down to children until all cards are dealt.
3. Select an object and say, "Turn over one card and put it in the center of the table. If your card is the same as this object, slap the table like this." Demonstrate.
4. Let children play, continuing to turn cards together. A child who slaps the table correctly collects the upturned cards. If two children slap the table on the same turn, let them devise a rule.
5. Repeat until all cards have been turned up.
6. Let children take leadership role.
7. Vary pictures and objects.

Variation

A set of pictures is substituted for the set of objects.

2.13 SAME-DIFFERENT PICTURES
GROUP SIZE: 2, 5

Behavioral Goals

1. Children label two or more pictures as the same or different.
2. Children select two or more pictures as the same or not the same.

Procedure

Materials

Select from such games as:

Lotto games

Baseball or Batman cards

Old Maid card game

Other playing card games

1. Help children label the pictures or cards.
2. See Lang. 4.12 for lotto games.
3. Participate initially as leader or dealer. Select a card from a pack and ask each child to select a card and to state whether it is the *same* as your card, or *not the same*, or *different*.

Variations

1. Let each child select and keep one card. Tell children cards are drawn in turn and they only keep cards that match the first card they drew.
2. Let two children play together. Give each child half the pack of cards.

   Place cards face down in front of each child. Tell children to turn over top cards simultaneously. One child keeps sets that are the *same*. The other child keeps sets that are *not the same*, or *different*. Let them decide who keeps each set.

Further Reference

Language 4.12

2.20 OBJECT PATTERNS
GROUP SIZE: 1, 2

Behavioral Goals

1. Children copy patterns of objects.
2. Children respond to and use such key language as color names, object labels, positional terms (first, next, last), row, and pattern.

Procedure

Materials

Sheet of construction paper

8 to 10 plastic spoons, all one color

9 to 10 plastic forks, same color as spoons

1. Invite a child to sit next to you on the same side of the table.
2. Make a row of alternating spoons and forks on a piece of paper and slide it in front of child, leaving a workspace directly in front of him.
3. Say, "Can you make a row just like mine?" The task is to use the same number of objects as is in the teacher's row.
4. If the child appears confused, say, "My row is spoon, fork, spoon, fork, spoon, fork," pointing to each object, always from left to right.
5. Check child's copy. Point to the first object in your row, on the left. Say, "Let's check: my first one is a spoon. Show me the first on your row. Is it a spoon?" Say, "Next comes a fork. Is your next one a fork?" Continue this until the last one. For the last one, say, "My last one is a fork."
6. If child loses his place in checking, help by having him point or touch.
7. After checking, say, "This is a spoon-fork pattern. Let's try another pattern."
8. Repeat steps 1 through 7 following the suggested order of patterns in Cog. Skills 2.21, as follows:
   a. Reverse single alternation pattern to be a fork-spoon pattern.
   b. Change to a double alternation pattern, as fork-fork-spoon-spoon.
   c. Reverse double alternation to a spoon-spoon-fork-fork pattern.
   d. Use 3 objects. For example, add straws to make a fork-straw-spoon pattern.
   e. Vary order of 3 objects.
   f. Change to 2-item alternating pattern with doubling of one item; for example, a spoon-spoon-fork-spoon-spoon-fork pattern.

Note: With each model, always state the pattern from left to right.

Cognitive Skills 2.20

Key Language

First	Next	Spoon
Last	Row	Fork
Pattern	Let's Check	Straw

Further Reference

Cognitive Skills 2.21, Item 1

CHART A: SUMMARY OF PATTERNING

Task	Teacher Materials	Child Materials	Pattern Sequence	No.
1. use miniature objects to copy a pattern of miniature objects	forks, spoons, and straws of one color	same as teacher	a. fork-spoon-fork-spoon b. fork-fork-spoon-spoon-fork-fork-spoon-spoon c. fork-fork-spoon-fork-fork-spoon d. fork-spoon-straw-fork-spoon-straw	2.20
2. use colored objects to copy a pattern of colored objects	colored cubes, poker chips in three colors	same as teacher	a. red-blue-red-blue b. red-red-blue-blue-red-red-blue-blue c. red-red-blue-red-red-blue d. red-white-blue-red-white-blue	2.22
3. use poker chips to copy patterns on a card	color pattern cards in three colors	poker chips	same as 2.22 above	2.23
4. use objects such as pegs, beads, and gummed shapes to copy color patterns on a card	color pattern cards in three colors	pegs and pegboard beads and pipe cleaners, gummed shapes, and construction paper	same as 2.22 above	2.23
5. fill in missing items in a pattern	color patterns of objects, such as cubes or pegs, with missing items	collection of objects, same as teacher set	same as 2.22 above	2.24
6. extend and create patterns	none	craft materials such as buttons, straws, paste, paper, and string	to be determined by teacher or child	2.24
7. make a pattern with letters or numerals	none	precut letters and numerals, letter and numeral stamps, typewriter	to be determined by child	2.24

Further Reference

Sociology 7.20–7.22
Language 4.21, 4.22
Mathematics 5.50

2.22 COLOR PATTERNS
GROUP SIZE: 1, 2

Behavioral Goal

Children copy a color pattern of objects.

Procedure

Materials

Poker chips

Cubes

Pegs and pegboards

Beads and pipe cleaners

2 or 3 colors, according to pattern

After children demonstrate mastery of tasks in 2.20, change tasks following Chart A, as follows:

1. Make a color pattern using cubes. For example: red, white, red, white, red, white, red, white.
2. Offer child box of cubes. Say, "Can you make a row just like mine?" The task is to use the same number of cubes as in the teacher's row.
3. Follow checking procedure in Cog. Skills 2.20. That is, say, "My first one is red. What color is your first one?" Continue checking from left to right across the row.
4. Have child touch each item. If child's row is a different length from the model row, say, "Your row is shorter (longer) than mine." Help child correct length.
5. Say, "This is a red-white pattern. Let's do another one."
6. Vary colors and number of cubes.
7. Introduce new patterns in the sequence suggested by Chart A, Cog. Skills 2.21.

Further Reference

Cognitive Skills 2.20, Chart A, 2.21, Item 2

2.23 COPYING PATTERN CARDS
GROUP SIZE: 1, 2, 5

Behavioral Goal

Children copy patterns from pattern cards.

Procedure

Materials

Pattern cards,[1] placing cards, and such materials as poker chips

Pegs and pegboards

Beads and pipe cleaners

Gummed shapes and construction paper

1. Give child a pattern card, a matching placing card, and a box of poker chips.
2. Ask child, "Can you make a copy of this pattern with poker chips?"
3. Help child check his pattern.
4. Independent activities.
    a. Ask two children to select pattern and placing cards, and the materials they wish to use. Ask them to help each other on checking.
    b. Ask two children to select one pattern and to copy that pattern in as many different materials as possible. See Item 4, Chart A, Cog. Skills 2.21.
    c. Follow Item 3, Chart A, Cog. Skills 2.21.
    d. For patterning with craft materials, see Soc. 7.21.

Further Reference

Sociology 7.20, 7.21
Chart A, Cognitive Skills 2.21

---

[1] A pattern card contains a row of squares patterned as to color, for example, red, white, red, white, red, white. A placing card contains a row of blank squares which may number 6, 8, or 9 squares.

2.24 COMPLETING, EXTENDING, AND CREATING PATTERNS
GROUP SIZE: 1, 2, 5

Behavioral Goals

1. Children fill in missing items in a pattern.
2. Children extend patterns.

Procedure

A. COMPLETING PATTERNS

Materials

Miniature objects

Cubes

Pegs and pegboards

Precut alphabet letters and numerals

Letter and numeral stamps

Typewriter

1. Prepare patterns with any of the above materials, depending on the child's interest and skill, leaving one or more gaps in the pattern. For example:
   a. An incomplete pattern with cubes or pegs
   Red Blue Red Blue   Blue Red Blue
   b. With alphabet letters
   A B A B A B   B A B
   c. With numerals
   3 3 4 4 3 3 4 3 4 4
2. Invite children to select an incomplete pattern and to complete it.
3. Invite children to help each other check their work.
4. Follow Item 5, Chart A, Cog. Skills 2.21.
5. See Soc. 7.21 for craft projects using incomplete patterns to be completed.

B. EXTENDING AND CREATING PATTERNS

Materials

Gummed shapes on construction paper

Beads on pipe cleaners

Buttons or straws pasted on paper

Paper chains

1. Teacher and children specify patterns to be used in craft projects for holidays or classroom use.
2. An example of pattern extension is: A red-green pattern is specified by teacher and children for making paper chains, and children extend this pattern as long as they wish.
3. Other examples of craft activities which can require extending patterns are decorating placemats, book covers, and spring hats; making bracelets, necklaces, and belts; room and tree decorations; decorating paper for gift wrap; potato printing.
4. Follow Items 5, 6, and 7 on Chart A, Cog. Skills 2.21.
5. See Soc. 7.20, 7.21, and 7.22 for additional suggestions.

Further Reference

Sociology 7.20, 7.21, 7.22
Chart A, Cognitive Skills 2.21

2.25 TRANSFORMING COLOR PATTERNS TO NONCOLOR DESIGNS

Behavioral Goal

Children transform color patterns to noncolor designs.

Procedure

Materials

Pattern card

Large and small gummed circles of 1 color

Circles and squares of 1 color

Round and square beads of 1 color

2 letter stamps

Contrasting textured paper

1. Give the child a pattern card such as red-blue-red-blue. Prepare one transformed pattern, by shape, such as a circle-square-circle-square pattern.
2. Tell child, "Here is a color pattern and a shape pattern. There is a way in which these patterns are alike." Hand child pipe cleaner and round and square green beads. Say, "Thread these beads on the pipe cleaner to make that kind of a pattern."
3. If child is confused, offer more practice with earlier structure models.

Further Reference

Chart A, Cognitive Skills 2.21

2.30 SORTING AND CLASSIFYING
GROUP SIZE: 2, 5

Behavioral Goals

1. Children sort concrete objects into groups and label the groups.
2. Children sort concrete objects into specified groups.
3. Children evidence understanding of grouping by completing a sorting of objects based on physical properties.

Procedure

Materials

Blocks

Block picture cards

1. Tape block picture cards to block shelves, to show exact size and shape of blocks to be stored on each shelf.
2. Help children sort and check their sorting of blocks at clean-up time. Label the blocks, saying, "All the doublongs go on this bottom shelf."

Variations

1. Establish routines at clean-up time to store like materials together. Use pictures or color or shape codes. Help children to check their sorting, to be sure that items are sorted correctly.
2. For further variations, see Sci. 6.40 and Soc. 7.20 and 7.21.

Further Reference

Science 6.40
Sociology 7.20 and 7.21

Music Structure Models

3.00	Goals in Music
3.09	Bibliography
3.10	Singing
3.11	Chants
3.12	Song with Movement
3.20	Rhythmic Movement with Percussion: Jump to Your Name
3.21	Clapping Rhythms
3.30	Movement: Same and Different Motions
3.31	Rhythmic Movement: Response to Beat, Form, Tempo, and Dynamics
3.32	Relating Movement to Pitch
3.33	Movement: Steady Beat
3.34	Movement: Melodic Pattern
3.40	Auditory Discrimination: Same and Different Tones, Voice and Xylophone
3.41	Auditory Discrimination: Same and Different Sounds of Percussion Instruments
3.42	Auditory Discrimination: Matching Xylophone Tones
3.43	Auditory Discrimination: Playing Instruments in Response to Their Sounds
3.50	Rhythm Instruments: Steady Beat
3.51	Rhythm Instruments: Improvisation

3.00 GOALS IN MUSIC

The young child's spontaneous enjoyment of music and movement is the base on which music concepts are built. This natural delight in musical activity is enhanced as the child begins to acquire some concepts of rhythm, tonality, accent, melody, mood, dynamics, phrasing, and timbre (tone color of different instruments). Musical experiences which contribute to development of these concepts include dance, movement, singing, listening and playing instruments.

Behavioral Goals

1. Children choose to participate in musical activities, including singing, movement, and listening to and playing rhythm and percussion instruments.
2. Children sing new and familiar songs and chants.
3. Children match singing tones with teacher and with each other.
4. Children produce contrasting singing tones on request, both higher and lower than given tones.
5. Children identify singing tones as matching (same) or different (higher or lower).
6. Children differentiate by specified responses between various single musical signals and between single and paired musical signals.
7. Children find the rhythmic patterns, steady beat and melody, of songs and chants by such responses as clapping, foot tapping, finger tapping, finger snapping, and thigh slapping (*patschen*), or the conductor's beat.
8. Children identify accent, phrasing, and timbre by such responses as clapping or dancing.
9. Children move to music, in patterned rhythmic responses, such as marching, galloping, or skipping.
10. Children move to music in free rhythmic response, with increasingly coordinated physical movements.
11. Children produce movements with music, appropriate to characterization, narrative, or mood of the music.
12. Children listen to music and identify, by specific responses, such musical elements as:
     a. Dynamics and tempo, as fast-slow, loud-soft, increasingly fast or slow, increasingly loud or soft;
     b. Melodic patterns (or rhythm of the melody), ascending and descending scalewise patterns, and repeated note patterns.

13. Children play rhythm instruments:
    a. Producing specified rhythmic patterns;
    b. Matching specified rhythmic patterns and tones;
    c. Accompanying songs, records, dances;
    d. Playing simple ensemble music.

3.09 BIBLIOGRAPHY AND SUGGESTED MUSICAL SOURCES

1. Seeger, Ruth C. 1948. *American Folk Songs for Children*, New York, Doubleday & Co.
2. Bailey, C. 1955. *Sing a Song with Charity Bailey*, New York, Plymouth Music Co.
3. Boni, Margaret B., and Lloyd, N. 1947. *Fireside Book of Folk Songs*, New York, Simon and Schuster.
4. Kapp, Paul. 1966. *Cock-a-doodle-do, Cock-a-doodle-dandy,* New York, Harper & Row.
5. 1952. *Music for Early Childhood*, Morristown, N. J., Silver, Burdett Co.
6. Krone, B., ed. 1959. *Music Across Our Country*, Chicago, Follett Publishing Co.
7. Landeck, B. 1950. *Songs to Grow On*, New York, Edward B. Marks Co.
8. Landeck, B., 1954. *More Songs to Grow On*, New York, Edward B. Marks and Wm. Sloane Associates.
9. Landeck, B., Crook, E., and Youngberg, H. C. 1964. *Making Music Your Own*, and Teacher's Edition 1 and 2, Morristown, N. J., Silver, Burdett Co.
10. Landeck, B. 1961. *Echoes of Africa in Folk Songs of the Americas*, New York, D. McKay Co.
11. Lomax, A. ed. 1964. *Penguin Book of American Folk Songs*, Baltimore, Md.
12. Ives, B. 1955. *At Home with Burl Ives*, New York, Leeds Music Corp.
13. Gamse, A., ed. 1964. *World's Favorite Hootenanny Sing Along Songs*, N. Y., Ashley Publications.

3.10 SINGING
GROUP SIZE: 5, ALL

Behavioral Goal

Children sing new and familiar songs.

Procedure

Materials

Records and phonograph

Piano and music books

Tape recorder and cassettes

Autoharp or guitar

Or nothing

1. Find out which songs children know and sing them daily until their song repertoire grows.
2. Introduce new songs regularly by singing them or playing them on tape, record, piano or otherwise.
    a. Sing or play a new song through several times, so that children will learn it by hearing and singing.
    b. If you are insecure in your own singing, rely on records, a musical instrument, or children who have reliable singing skills, or ask another teacher who sings well to tape record the new song.
    c. If a new song presents rhythmic difficulty, see Music 3.33 for establishing the steady beat of a song.
3. Initiate singing at any time you like or when children start to sing. Facilitate routines, or nonroutine walks, by singing.
4. Seek opportunities to encourage singing or to introduce songs in such activites as block play, carpentry, housekeeping play, cooking with clay, outdoor play with balls, bicycles and walking boards, and on walking or bus trips.

5. Seek variety in songs, to include:

Familiar and unfamiliar songs	Action songs and finger plays
Popular music	Folk dance songs
Folk songs of varied ethnic origins	Nursery rhyme songs
Classical music	Songs composed by teacher or children
Ditties	Songs from light opera music
Teacher or child-composed words to familiar songs	Songs from opera music
Patriotic songs	Songs from modern music
Foreign language songs, featuring variety of languages	

6. See Music 3.09 for suggested musical sources.
7. For records, see *Schwann Catalogue*, available from library or record store.

Further Reference

Music 3.09, 3.33

3.11 CHANTS
GROUP SIZE: 5, ALL

Behavioral Goals

1. Children match teacher's musical tones.
2. Children produce their own chants.
3. Children use correct names for colors and articles of clothing.
4. Children use selected standard syntactic forms. See Lang. 4.14.
5. Children sing about themselves—the colors and articles of their clothing.
6. Children enjoy being the focus of class attention. See Soc. 7.11.

Procedure

1. Sing a chant, mentioning the color of at least one article of clothing of each child. For example, "John has a white shirt. Mary has red shoes. James has a brown belt." Sing a descending minor third, a monotone, or any other simple melodic line. Example of descending minor third: B flat-G, or any other similar interval.
2. Vary the chants to include:
   a. Monotone chants;
   b. Sing monotone chant on different notes;
   c. Ascending or descending scalewise chants;
   d. Chants which ascend or descend by thirds or fifths (for example, to ascend by thirds, sing C—E—G; to ascend by fifths, sing C—G.
   e. Varieties of tone patterns;
   f. Varied rhythms.
3. Ask each child to sing with you, or to chant after you about his clothes.
4. Ask each child to make up his own chant about his clothes and help the group to match his chant.
5. Teach song, "Mary Wore A Red Dress," substituting names of children in class. For recording, see Folkways FC 7020, "School Days."
6. Find content for chants in material such as:
   a. Children's family composition;
   b. Children's activities in class;
   c. Children's preferences for food, color, or games;
   d. Children's recollections of the high points of trip;
   e. Children's products in class.

Further Reference

Language 4.14
Sociology 7.11

3.12 SONG WITH MOVEMENT
GROUP SIZE: 5, ALL

Behavioral Goals

Music:
1. Children learn words and music of song.
2. Children produce appropriate movements, with large, free motions.

Language:
1. Children associate correct labels with body parts, by physical movement. See Lang. 4.13.
2. Children make up new rhymes, appropriate to song. See Lang. 4.80.
3. Children sing selected standard syntactic forms. See Lang. 4.14.

Procedure

Materials

Record, "Put Your Finger in the Air"

Song without record

Other song naming parts of the body

1. Teach song by singing it several times, demonstrating movements.
2. Encourage children to sing along and match your movements.
3. Help children to learn song well, pronounce labels clearly, and offer appropriate movements.
4. Ask individual children to lead song, and to make up words using labels not previously used, as, "Put your toe in the dough," or "Put your knee in the sea." Mention that these are rhymes. See Lang. 4.80 for further rhyming.
5. Use other songs or recordings which name parts of the body, such as, "Monkey See, Monkey Do," and "Hokey-Pokey."
6. Invent new words to songs, or encourage children to help invent new words, in order to use some of the standard syntactic forms in Lang. 4.14.

Further Reference

Language 4.13, 4.14, 4.80

3.20 RHYTHMIC MOVEMENT WITH PERCUSSION: JUMP TO YOUR NAME
GROUP SIZE: 5, ALL

Behavioral Goals

Music:
1. Children jump rhythmically to drumbeat pattern of names.
2. Children demonstrate sense of beat.
3. Children relate jumping to soft-loud dynamics of drumbeat.

Physical Control:
1. Children make free physical responses.
2. Children control physical movement in response to such signals as a drumbeat and a verbal signal.

Self-knowing:
Children use full names and full names of other children and adults in the class. See Soc. 7.11.

Procedure

Materials

Drum and beater

1. Demonstrate procedure. Beat drum rhythmically and jump, while chanting your own name several times, as, "Mrs. Brown, Mrs. Brown, Mrs. Brown."
2. Ask one child at a time to jump to his name. When you stop beating the drum, add a verbal signal. "Now sit down."
3. Adjust the drumbeat to child's jumping rhythm, whether fast or slow, until child demonstrates ability to follow drumbeat.
4. Later, expect child to follow the drumbeat.
5. Vary the dynamics of the drumbeat, loud-soft, and the tempo, fast-slow.
6. Emphasize physical control, asking child, "Did you sit down when I sang 'Now sit down'?"
7. Later, omit verbal signal of "Now sit down." Offer feedback to children, as, "You stopped jumping when the drum stopped," "You jumped faster than my drum."

8. Add a further variation. When you chant and beat the rhythm of your name, all children jump with you. Otherwise, only one child jumps at a time, as before, to his own name.
9. Give more advanced children turns controlling the drum and calling names of other children.
10. As more children show control, allow children to pass the drum around the circle as each child completes his turn to be caller.
11. Develop these procedures slowly over a period of several months, accepting and adapting to the rate at which children develop these skills.

Further Reference

Sociology 7.00

3.21 CLAPPING RHYTHMS
GROUP SIZE: 5, ALL

Behavioral Goals

1. Children copy and produce rhythmic patterns by clapping.
2. Children transform rhythmic patterns from one action to another, and from action to language.

Procedure

1. Invite several children to join you in a clapping game.
2. Produce simple brief rhythmic patterns, with no more than 5 claps, such as 2 long and 2 short claps.
3. Repeat the pattern several times, inviting children to join you by gesture rather than verbally, to maintain a brisk pace.
4. Try out a variety of patterns, such as:
Long-Short-Short
Long-Long-Short-Short-Short
Short-Short-Short-Long-Long
5. Invite each child by gesture to reproduce a pattern individually.
6. As children demonstrate skill in copying patterns, encourage them to produce their own patterns.
7. Invite children to lead clapping patterns by producing a pattern for other children to copy.

Variations

1. Repeat preceding procedures, adding any percussion instrument to accompany or lead the clapping activity.
2. Substitute for hand clapping such actions as foot tapping, finger snapping, patschen (thigh slapping), or stamping.
3. Transformation 1: Demonstrate a transformation from one action to another, by clapping a rhythmic pattern and then foot tapping the same pattern.
4. Transformation 2: Demonstrate a transformation from an action to a chanting pattern, for example, by foot tapping a pattern and then chanting it, singing "la-la-la." Invite children to make similar transformations.
5. Transformation 3: Demonstrate a transformation from an action or chant to a verbal pattern. For example, chant "la-la-la," then chant a sentence to the same rhythmic pattern, such as, "I want milk." Invite children to make similar transformations.

3.30 MOVEMENT: SAME AND DIFFERENT MOTIONS
GROUP SIZE: 5, ALL

Behavioral Goals

Music:
Children produce appropriate movements to words of song, and match other children's movements.

Cognitive skills:
Children copy movements, when asked to make *same* motion, or produce *different* movement when asked to. See Cog. Skills 2.11.

Procedure

Materials

None (unless teacher wishes to play a recording)

1. Teach song, "If You're Happy and You Know It," or "Did You Ever See a Lassie," by singing it and demonstrating movement, several times.
2. Ask group to do same motions as you do. Help children, if necessary.
3. As children learn the words, call on each child to make a motion. Ask group to copy same movement.
4. Gradually emphasize a *change*, saying, "John made this motion," demonstrating it. "Now, Sharon, show us a *different* one."
5. Ask group, "What did Mary do? What did John do? Did Sharon do the *same* motion that John did?" Elicit, "No, it was *different*."
6. Use other songs such as "The Mulberry Bush," "All Around the Kitchen," "Let Everyone Clap Hands Like Me."

Further Reference

Cognitive Skills 2.11

3.31 RHYTHMIC MOVEMENT: RESPONSE TO BEAT, FORM, TEMPO, AND DYNAMICS
GROUP SIZE: ALL

Behavioral Goals

Music:
1. Children walk and relate arm movements to beat of music.
2. Children make different physical responses to parts 1 and 2 of 2-part musical form of song.
3. Children adapt to changes of tempo, fast-slow, and dynamics, loud-soft, in movement and song.

Sociology:
Children exchange handshakes with other children as neighbors, or members of the class. See Soc. 7.13.

Procedure

Materials

Drum

Song or recording of "Ride Away on Your Horses"

Adequate space for free movement of group

1. Introduce song. Say, "Here's a song about riding on ponies. You may ride anywhere in this room as we sing."
2. Sing first part several times with the children and "ride" around the room with them.
3. Tell children, "That was the first part. Now the song changes. Listen." Model handshaking procedure as you sing the second part.
4. Complete song, modeling action.
5. When children have learned song and actions, introduce variations, such as:
    a. "Ride Away in Your Autos;"
    b. "Fly Away in Your Airplanes;"
    c. Elicit suggestions for further variations from children.
6. Follow similar procedure for different songs, such as "Did You Ever See a Lassie."

7. Words of song, "Ride Away on Your Horses":

    Part 1
    Ride away on your ponies,
    Your ponies, your ponies.
    Ride away on your ponies.
    Whoa, whoa, whoa.

    Part 2
    Stop a moment just to say,
    How do you do on this lovely day?
    How do you do on this lovely day?
    Then off we go—oh.

3.32 RELATING MOVEMENT TO PITCH
GROUP SIZE: 5, ALL

Behavioral Goals

1. Children relate movement to low and high pitch.
2. Children adjust movement to changes in tempo.
3. Children respond to positional terms. See Geog. 8.10.

Procedure

Materials

Drum

Bells or triangle

1. Describe game of Jack-in-the-Box. Say, "When I play the drum, see how low on the floor you can get. Keep your head down low while I play the drum. When I play the bells, jump up or dance any way you like. As soon as I play the drum again, get down on the floor just as low as you can get."
2. Play drum, chanting, "Jack-in-the-Box, you're down so low, you're asleep in your box when I tell you so." Maintain a distinct rhythm.
3. Play bells, chanting, "Jack, go fly, up high, in the sky, so high."
4. Repeat Steps 2 and 3.
5. Later, play the drum and bells, without chanting, relying on musical signals alone.
6. Change tempo—slower, faster.
7. Later, ask a child to play the instrument and be the caller.

Variations

1. Use the same instruments. Associate the drum sound with an airplane motor warming up on the ground and the bell with the airplane flying in the air. Ask children to make appropriate movements as you gradually change tempo and instrument use.
2. Use different instruments for such actions as climbing a ladder, walking upstairs, climbing a mountain, ascending in an elevator. Always associate the higher pitch with physical height.
3. Drop verbal signals as soon as children appear ready to respond to musical signals alone.

Further Reference

Geography 8.10

41

3.33 MOVEMENT: STEADY BEAT
GROUP SIZE: ALL

Behavioral Goal

Children mark the steady beat by movement or by playing rhythm instruments.

Procedure

Materials

Records or piano music or singing

Rhythm instruments

1. Use song or recording of music with strongly marked rhythm. For example, songs such as:
   "Don't You Push Me Down"
   "Skip to My Lou"
   "I'll Race You Down the Mountain"
   "Old Joe Clarke"
   "She'll Be Coming Round the Mountain"
   "Shoo Fly, Don't Bother Me"
   "Drill Ye Tarriers, Drill"
   Also use recordings of such music as square dance music, popular music, Indian songs, marches, Italian tarantellas, minuets, and ethnic folk music.
2. Sing the song or hum the music, demonstrating a way to mark the steady beat by clapping softly, inviting the children to join in.
3. Ask children to suggest other ways to mark the steady beat. Other possibilities are:
   a. Foot tapping;
   b. Finger tapping;
   c. Thigh slapping;
   d. Head shaking;
   e. Finger snapping;
   f. Mouth clicking;
   g. Hand waving;
   h. Conductor's beat.
4. Model moving to mark the steady beat, inviting children to join you (for example, marching).

5. Invite children to find individual ways to move, to mark the steady beat. Feature individual variations.
6. Offer children rhythm instruments to mark the steady beat.

Further Reference

Myers, Louis K. 1961. *Teaching Children Music in the Elementary School* Englewood Cliffs, N. J., Prentice-Hall.

3.34 MOVEMENT: RHYTHM OF MELODIC PATTERN[1]
GROUP SIZE: ALL

Behavioral Goals

1. Children find the steady beat of a song.
2. Children produce relaxed, free movements to song, as they sing.
3. Children find the rhythm of melodic pattern of a song by specific movements.

Procedure

Materials

None, unless teacher chooses to use a recording. (Song may be "Once There Was a Shepherdess," a French folk song with a melodic pattern that is suggestive of skipping or swaying, or any other song with a clear melodic pattern. The words may be changed to relate to a holiday or seasonal event as suggested below.)

1. Teach song to group by singing it several times with them, or start with a song children already know. Before Thanksgiving, when there is a real pumpkin or a picture of a pumpkin in the room, change the words of "Once There Was a Shepherdess" to:
   I'm going to choose a pumpkin,
   So big and round
   And down on the ground.
   I'm going to choose a pumpkin
   So big and fat and round.
   Or use this verse:
   I want to choose a turkey,
   Tender and sweet
   With lots of meat.
   I want to choose a turkey
   For Thanksgiving dinner.
   Or make up your own verse, with the children's help.
2. Ask children to crouch on the floor and pretend to be pumpkins. Sing the song, moving about the room making free movements, demonstrating a way to accent the melodic pattern of the song. At the end of the song, choose two "pumpkins," touching them lightly, saying, "Join me." These two children join you, singing the song and moving freely to accent the melodic pattern. Repeat the song several times, until all "pumpkins" are dancing.

3. Other songs with clear melodic patterns which may be used for free movement include "Ride Away on Your Horses," "I Could Have Danced All Night" (from *My Fair Lady*), "Shall We Dance?" (from *The King and I*), "As I Walked Out on the Streets of Laredo," "Get Along, Little Dogies," and "Red Leaves Falling Down."

4. Change to classical music, such as:

    a. Debussy's *Children's Corner* music;

    b. "Brother, Will You Dance With Me" from the opera, *Hansel and Gretel*;

    c. Stravinsky's *Firebird Music*, or *Rite of Spring*;

    d. Haydn's symphonies, such as the *Surprise Symphony*, the *Toy Symphony*, or the *Hen Symphony*;

    e. Any Mozart symphony, Third Movement Minuet;

    f. Grieg's *Peer Gynt Suite*, or *Norwegian Dances*;

    g. Dvorak's *New World Symphony*, or *Slavonic Dances*.

---

[1] Rhythm of melodic pattern refers to the rhythm of the notes which compose the melody or tune of the song.

3.40 AUDITORY DISCRIMINATION: SAME AND DIFFERENT TONES, VOICE AND XYLOPHONE
GROUP SIZE: 1, 2, 5

Behavioral Goals

1. Children match singing tones, call them *same*.
2. Children offer *different* tones from what they hear.
3. Children match a xylophone tone to another xylophone tone.
4. Children find a *different* tone on the xylophone from the tone they hear.

Procedure

Materials

Two xylophones

Two beaters

1. Matching singing tones.
   a. Sing a phrase such as, "Good morning," on one tone and ask child to match *same* note. As children's skill grows, ask a child to sing a note and another child to match it. Gradually, ask the group to decide if the two notes (tones) are the *same*.
   b. When tone matching becomes skillful, ask for *different* tones. Sing phrase on one note and ask for a different tone. Later, ask a child to sing a phrase on one note and another child to sing it back on a different tone, and the group to decide whether the two tones are different.
   c. Use a pitchpipe, piano, set of resonator bells, or other melodic instrument to play the two notes to help children hear their different tones. Or tape record the sequence and replay the recording, to keep the tones in the children's immediate memory.
2. Matching xylphone tones.
   a. Play a note on one xylophone and ask a child to match the tone on the second xylophone.
   b. Later, ask a child to play a note on one xylophone, another child to match it on the second xylophone, and the group to decide whether the tones are the *same*.
   c. Later, ask for different tones, as in matching and contrasting singing notes above.
   d. When featuring different tones, start with gross differences in pitch, such as fifths (C–G), then gradually move to thirds (C–E), seconds (C–D), and finally to half-tones (C–C sharp).

3.41 AUDITORY DISCRIMINATION: SAME-DIFFERENT SOUNDS OF PERCUSSION INSTRUMENTS
GROUP SIZE: 1, 2, 5

Behavioral Goals

1.   Children make physical response to musical percussion signal.
2.   Children make a physical response to one signal and *different* response to a second signal.
3.   Children make a physical response to one signal and *different* response to paired signals.
4.   Children respond to single and paired musical sounds by use of pictures.

Procedure

Materials

   Percussion instruments

   Pictures or sketches of the same instruments

   Duplicate sketches of the instrument used, such as xylophone, drum, triangle, rhythm sticks, tambourine; make enough copies for whole class

1.   Motor response to single sound.
   a.   Play one percussion instrument which children see, and request children to make the same response to the sound every time they hear it, such as, "Clap your hands."
   b.   Play same instrument, which children *cannot* see, requesting same response. Say, "Remember what you do when you hear this sound? What do you do? Show me."
   c.   Repeat *a* and *b* with a different instrument, requesting another response such as, "Tap your foot when you hear this sound. This sound is different."
2.   Motor response to single and paired sounds.
   a.   Establish two new responses, one for a single sound (as the drum) and the other for a paired sound (as the drum and xylophone played simultaneously). "When you hear the drum by itself, clap your hands. When you hear the drum and xylophone together, jump." Children can see the instruments as you play them.
   b.   Follow same procedure as in 2*a*, but hide the instruments.

3. Picture selection response to single and paired sounds.
    a. Show picture of each of two instruments you will play, such as drum and tambourine. Give each child a copy of each picture, naming the instruments.
    b. Ask children to hold up the picture of the instruments they hear. First, play the instruments within sight of the children, then out of sight. Play each instrument by itself, and both together, at random.
    c. Give children teacher role.

3.42 AUDITORY DISCRIMINATION: MATCHING XYLOPHONE TONES
GROUP SIZE: 5, ALL

Behavioral Goals

1. Children match xylophone tones in a scalewise melody.
2. Children improvise words for this melody, as a variation on the rhymes learned. See Lang. 4.80.
3. Children accompany song on rhythm sticks or bells, singing and playing alternate phrases.

Procedure

Materials

Xylophone

Rhythm sticks

Bells   ·

1. Introduce the activity by leading the group to review some nursery rhymes they know, such as "Jack and Jill," or "Humpty Dumpty."
2. Say, "Here's another rhyme on the xylophone." Sing:
   One, one, one—this is *fun*.
   Two, two, two—what shall we *do?*
   Three, three, three—sing alone with *me*.
   Four, four, four—let's play some *more*.
   Play the xylophone, starting on the first note, which is C, as you sing it.
3. Help children practice this song, with your xylophone accompaniment. Later, let children take turns playing the xylophone accompaniment.
4. Later, sing the numbers only, asking children to respond with the rhymes.
5. Later, boys sing numbers and girls sing rhymes, or vice versa, as one child plays xylophone.
6. Encourage children to improvise new and different rhymes, accepting *all* suggestions of real rhymes, including nonsense syllables.

Further Reference

Language 4.80

3.43 AUDITORY DISCRIMINATION: PLAYING INSTRUMENTS IN RESPONSE TO THEIR SOUNDS
GROUP SIZE: 5, ALL

Behavioral Goals

1. Children distinguish timbre of different rhythm instruments by playing the one they hear.
2. Children respond to the changes in dynamics they hear.

Procedure

Materials

Drums

Bells or triangles

1. Review with children a well-known song, such as, "Let Everyone Clap Hands Like Me."
2. Hand drums and bells to a few children. Say, "If I play the bells when I sing the first part, then children who have bells play the part with me. If I play the drum, when I sing the second part, then children who have a drum play the second part with me."
3. Sing, "Let everyone play just like me," using bells, then drum.
4. Have children exchange instruments so that each child has a turn with drums and bells.
5. Introduce dynamics variations. Say, "If I play my drum softly, you must drum softly. If I play my bells loud, you play loud, too."
6. When children become skillful, introduce a further variation by hiding the instruments so that children respond to auditory cues alone.
7. Give children the teacher role later.

**3.50 RHYTHM INSTRUMENTS: STEADY BEAT
GROUP SIZE: 5, ALL**

Behavioral Goal

Children play instruments rhythmically in steady beat.

Procedure

Materials

Rhythm instruments

1. Review the song to be used, such as "Let Everyone Clap Hands Like Me," asking children to sing and clap the steady beat. Steady beat refers to the basic rhythm which is a clock-like regular pattern, irrespective of the melody.
2. Ask children to, "Clap just like me—softly when I clap softly, loudly when I clap loudly."
3. Let children select rhythm instruments. Say, "This time we'll play our instruments instead of clapping. If I play bells, you play *only* if you have bells. If I play the drum, play *only* if you have a drum.
4. Ask children to exchange instruments, later, so that each child tries more than one instrument.

3.51 RHYTHM INSTRUMENTS: IMPROVISATION
GROUP SIZE: 5, ALL

Behavioral Goals

1. Children produce rhythmic patterns on instruments.
2. Children improvise patterns on instruments.

Procedure

Materials

Rhythm instruments

1. Demonstrate by playing on the drum, as you describe a new game. Say, "Here's the rhythm of my name." Beat the drum to the rhythmic pattern of your name. Later, play the pattern and ask children to identify it.
2. Ask children to drum their own name patterns, and later, each other's.
3. Invite children to practice this game, with different instruments.
4. Invite children to find more ways to play each instrument. For example, a drum may be played on its head or side.
5. Later, give children teacher role to beat rhythms of nursery rhymes, chants, or songs.
6. Invite children to improvise on rhythm instruments.

Language

4.00   Goals in Language
4.10   Eliciting and Extending Spontaneous Language
4.101   Listening to Stories and Books
4.11   Tape Recording Children's Speech
4.12   Practicing Present Tense of To Have
4.13   Using Precise Labels: Ring and Play Game
4.14   Selected Syntactic Forms in Standard English: Reference List
4.15   Word Games: Negation
4.16   Word Games: Transformation from Predicate to Noun Phrase
4.17   Word Games: Transformation from Verb to Noun and to Noun Phrase
4.18   Practicing Pronoun Use
4.19   Word Games: Verbs—3rd Person Singular
4.20   Name Recognition and Replication Without Writing
4.21   Procedures for Use of Primer Typewriter
4.22   Manuscript Writing
4.50   Model Dialogue Using Puppets to Practice Negation
4.60   Phonics: Sound-Symbol Relationships
4.61   Beginning Reading: Adapted Linguistic Method
4.62   Sample Initial Decoding Instruction
4.621   Word List for Teacher Reference
4.63   Sample Initial Sight Word Instruction
4.64   Making and Reading Booklets
4.80   Rhyming Words and Nonsense Syllables
4.90   Creative Dramatization

4.00 GOALS IN LANGUAGE

The young child's oral language is the base for all his language learning. The language program follows a sequence which begins with eliciting free flow of children's natural speech without interruption, correction, or judgment. All content areas of the program contribute suggestions for cognitive uses of language and forms of vocabulary expansion, use, and development. In addition, specific procedures are listed to foster practice with standard English speech forms, auditory discrimination, and learning to read and write letters and numerals as well as simple words and sentences.

Many children speak an English dialect which may be different from the standard English dialect taught in school. In this program, the child's native English dialect is accepted and respected. The standard English dialect is taught as a second dialect, a school form, through games.

Behavioral Goals

1. Children respond in appropriate nonverbal forms to verbal requests and instructions.
2. Children respond verbally to verbal requests and instructions.
3. Children initiate verbal communication of needs, requests, questions, and comments.
4. Children narrate class experiences in sequence.
5. Children use precise name labels and descriptive terms.
6. Children produce selected standard syntactic forms.
7. Children recognize and produce rhymes, and improvise nonsense rhymes.
8. Children dramatize and narrate stories.
9. Children enjoy hearing stories read.
10. Children recognize their names.
11. Children replicate names with precut alphabet letters.
12. Children write names, and other words and letters, and typewrite them.
13. Children identify and write letters of the alphabet, upper and lower case.
14. Children identify and differentiate among specified speech sounds.
15. Children associate speech sounds with alphabet letters.
16. Children read and write sentences and stories.
17. Children use positional terms in writing.
18. Children follow rules of word games.

4.10 ELICITING AND EXTENDING SPONTANEOUS LANGUAGE
GROUP SIZE: 2, 5

Behavioral Goals

1. Children talk spontaneously as they work and play.
2. Children label materials and use descriptive words as they participate in play activites.

Procedure

Materials

Salt	Food coloring
Flour	Mixing bowl
Water	

1. Place materials on table and invite children to help make playdough.
2. Help children label materials as they use them.
3. Help children put two cups flour and one cup salt into mixing bowl and encourage children to feel the dry mixture.
4. Help children add colored water, a little bit at a time. Have children take turns stirring the mixture.
5. Use words supplied by children and offer synonyms as needed.
6. As children increase their spontaneous speech, decrease verbal participation.

Key Language

Flour	Dry
Salt	White
Water	Powdery
Coloring	Sticky
Color names	Mixture
Soft	Cup
Smooth	

Note: Other examples of activities which elicit children's spontaneous speech are clay modeling, block play, housekeeping play and water play.

4.101 LISTENING TO STORIES AND BOOKS
GROUP SIZE: 1, 2, 5

Behavioral Goal

Children choose to listen to stories and books read by teachers.

Procedure

Materials

Stories composed by children on the basis of common school experiences

Stories dictated by individual children

Trade books

Tape recorder and cassettes

1. Keep story reading groups small and arrange for occasional listening experiences on an individual basis.
2. Respect children's right to decide whether or not they choose to listen to the story or book that the teacher chooses.
3. Give children opportunities to select the book or story they would like to hear.
4. Avoid reading to children when classroom noises are at a high level. At such times, offer children tape recordings and headsets.
5. Elicit children's contributions to the story or comments about the story or the pictures.
6. Explain meanings of new words in context, inject explanatory material whenever you sense a need, and, if you think it might be helpful, add occasional brief summaries or ask questions to involve the listener, such as, "What do you think will happen next?" or "What will he do now?"
7. Discuss the story after you read it, involving the children in recalling the sequence of the story and, where applicable, speculating about possible alternatives, with such questions as, "What would you have done?"

Further Reference

Language 4.11

4.11 TAPE RECORDING CHILDREN'S SPEECH
GROUP SIZE: 1, 2, 5, ALL

Behavioral Goals

1. Children produce language freely for tape recording.
2. Children recognize their own voices on recorded tape.
3. Children narrate classroom experiences in sequence.
4. Children listen to and elaborate on recorded speech.

Procedure

Materials

Tape recorder and tape

Foam rubber sponge

1. Recording Spontaneous Speech
   a. Cup microphone with foam rubber sponge to minimize noise. Fasten sponge with rubber band.
   b. Place microphone in a likely place to pick up conversations of children at play. Avoid noisy areas such as block building. Make recordings in dramatic play, or in manipulative play areas.
   c. Offer the children an opportunity to listen to the tape soon after the recording is completed. Encourage repetitive listening. Since experience indicates that children tend to become self-corrective in language production, offer no teacher correction.
2. Recording Planned Verbalization
   a. Group recording:
      (1) Record group chants, nursery rhymes and songs. Replay tape immediately. Invite individual children to record the same materials and to listen to their recordings.
      (2) Record creative dramatization by children for replay. See Lang. 4.90.
   b. Individual recording:
      (1) Invite interested children to tape record stories about their own art work, about books, or realistic experiences, and to hear replays.
      (2) Invite interested children to narrate class experiences in sequence for replay and verification, with assistance from other children and teachers.

Further Reference

Language 4.90

4.12 PRACTICING PRESENT TENSE OF "TO HAVE"
GROUP SIZE: 2, 5

Behavioral Goal

Children practice using simple sentences requiring the present tense of the verb *to have.*

Procedure

A. A LOTTO GAME

Materials

A lotto game

1. Demonstrate procedure by being caller.
2. Say, "This game has rules. The caller has to hold up a picture card and say, 'Who has this picture?' If you have the same picture on your card, you say, 'I have it.'"
3. Continue calling pictures, without requiring model sentences from children.
4. Later, appoint each child in turn to be the caller, reminding him of the rules. If the caller forgets the verbal rule, or uses a nonstandard form, such as "who have" instead of "who has," quietly rephrase the sentence in standard form, without requiring the child to repeat it and without slowing the game. Experience indicates that children soon pick up the standard form by themselves.

B. AN OBJECT GAME

Materials

Box of attractive objects, such as:

Miniature animals

Synthetic fruit

Miniature vehicles

1. Show children contents of box and let them handle the objects.
2. Demonstrate rules of game. Pick object out of box and hide it, without letting anyone see it.
3. Say, "Guess what I have!" Give each child a turn to guess, suggesting that he say, "You have a _____."
4. Respond either positively or negatively, as "Yes, I have a _____." Give player the object that he has guessed.

4.13 USING PRECISE LABELS: RING AND PLAY GAME
GROUP SIZE: 2, 5

Behavioral Goals

1. Children respond to precise labels and descriptive terms.
2. Children use precise labels and descriptive terms.
3. Children respond in appropriate nonverbal form to instruction.

Procedure

A. TEACHER PREPARATION

Materials

Two identical sets of about 10 attractive objects, such as:

Red miniature car	2 blue plastic buttons, one large and one small
Green counting cube	Small doll
Pink plastic spoon	Plastic carrot
White plush rabbit	Plastic cow
Aluminum pot	Tape recorder and cassette

1. Prepare 2 boxes of materials.
2. Make tape recording of game for children to play, as you play it with children for the first time.

B. CONTENT OF RECORDING

1. Tape record the rules of the game. Use such language as, "Each of you has a box. It's closed. Wait until you hear a bell to open it. Remember, your box is closed. In this game, when I name something in your box, you take it out. Are you ready? Let's go!"
2. Ring the bell. Name each object in the box. Say, "Find the red car." Establish a slow pace by five-second pauses. Ring the bell before the next name is called.
3. At the end of the naming game, instruct players to return objects to box *in order to play another game*.
4. For second game, restate the rule in this way: "This time I will tell something about one thing in your box. You find it. Are you ready? Wait for the bell!"
5. Ring the bell. Use descriptive terms of color, texture, shape, or size. Say, "Find the red object. Find something soft and furry." Or, "Find something smooth and shiny." As before, pace the words slowly, using a bell sound to signal the end of the pause.

Language 4.13

<u>*Variations*</u>

Materials

Same as above without tape recorder

1. Three children play the game without tape recorder, taking turns as caller or leader.

Materials

Pictures of objects

2. With more advanced children, substitute pictures for objects.

Materials

Word cards

3. For beginning readers, substitute word cards for names of objects.

4.14 REFERENCE LIST (to be used with Lang. 4.15 through 4.19, and where cited)

Selected Syntactic Forms in Standard English for playful practice in stories, chants, and puppet dialogues.

To help children who speak a nonstandard English dialect, the following list of syntactic forms was selected as containing the important ones to practice. It is *not* intended to suppress children's spontaneous native speech. Practice in standard forms *is* expected to establish familiarity with this syntax for reading purposes.

	Syntactic Form	Standard Form	A Dialect Form
1.	Yes-no questions with main verbs	Did he go?	He went?
2.	*Wh*-questions[1] with main verbs	Why did he go?	Why he went?
3.	Use of single tense marker	He didn't tear it.	He didn't tore it.
4.	Separability of *am* from *I*	Am I next?	Is I'm next?
5.	Third person singular—*s*	He has. He comes. He does.	He have. He come. He do.
6.	Possessives	Their book Mary's hat In our house In her house	They book Mary hat In we house In she house
7.	Regular past tense with *-ed*	I walked.	I walk.
8.	*Didn't* instead of *ain't*	He didn't go.	He ain't go.
9.	Single instead of double negatives	He might never go.	He might not never go.

[1] Wh = why, where, when, who, what.

4.15 WORD GAMES: NEGATION
GROUP SIZE: 5

Behavioral Goals

1. Children practice producing selected syntactic forms.
2. Children follow rules of word games.
3. Children make transformation from positive to negative statements.

Procedure

Materials

Box of attractive and colorful objects, such as:

Pair of red shoes, doll size

Miniature blue car

Synthetic banana

White ball

String of pink beads

A. NEGATE NAME OF OBJECT

1. Show children contents of box and let them handle the objects.
2. Ask one child to select one object and say what it is, as, "This is a blue car." Accept incomplete sentences.
3. Model a question which requires a negative response, such as, "Is that an elephant?"
4. Accept child's response and rephrase, if necessary, to, "No, it is not an elephant."
5. Ask a few more questions, then give children turns to ask questions. Keep on modeling the negative response, without asking children to repeat it.
6. Variation: Chant the question as well as the model answer, such as, "Is that an elephant? It is not an elephant."
7. Distribute miniature animals. Have each child chant about the animal he receives.

B. NEGATE THE COLOR OF THE OBJECT

Chant the question and answer, as, "Is that a red one? It is not a red one."

C. "GUESS WHAT I HAVE" GAME

    1. Model the rules by picking an object from the box, hiding it behind your back and asking, "Guess what I have? It is not a _____ (for example, purple elephant)."

    2. Respond to wrong guesses with, "It is not a _____."

    3. Tell a child to select an object, to play the game.

4.16 WORD GAMES: TRANSFORMATION FROM PREDICATE TO NOUN PHRASE
GROUP SIZE: 5, 1

Behavioral Goals

1. Children practice producing selected standard syntactic forms.
2. Children follow rules of word games.
3. Children make transformation from predicate to noun phrase.
4. Children indicate understanding of transformation from predicate to noun phrase by crayoning duplicated pictures.

Procedure

Materials

One deck of cards in black and white showing objects children will know

One deck of blank cards in various colors

1. Model the game by drawing one card from each deck. Say, "This is blue and this is a truck. Together, they make a blue truck." (This is a model transformation from predicate to noun phrase.)
2. Tell children to take turns playing the game. Each player keeps his cards.
3. Sort and reshuffle the cards, to play the game again.

Variations for Independent Activity

Materials

Same as above and one duplicated sheet for each child with object pictures the same as in the picture deck of cards

1. Tell child to take a duplicated sheet, crayons and the two decks of cards.
2. Tell him to play the game as before, this time crayoning the pictures on the duplicated sheet, instead of verbalizing.

4.17 WORD GAMES: TRANSFORMATION FROM VERB TO NOUN AND TO NOUN PHRASE
GROUP SIZE: 5, ALL

Behavioral Goals

1. Children practice producing selected syntactic forms.
2. Children follow rules of word games.
3. Children make transformation from verb to noun.
4. Children make transformation from verb to noun phrase.

Procedure

Materials

Box of objects that suggest action to children, such as:

Drum	Microphone or picture of one
Synthetic fruit	Cup, bowl and spoon
Flag	Book

1. Action Game with Objects—Verb to Noun
   a. Invite a small group to play an action game.
   b. Tell one child to select one object from the box and to do something with the object.
   c. Tell the group to guess, "What is he doing?"
   d. Rephrase children's responses, if needed, to the present progressive form of the verb, as, "He is eating." Other actions might be talking, singing, drinking, drumming, waving, reading.
   e. Initiate a chant, to establish the transformation from verb to noun, as, "He is eating. He is an eater."
   f. Give children turns to select an object and to initiate an action and proceed as above.
2. Action Game Without Objects—Verb to Noun Proceed as in Step 1, except that no objects are used and each child takes a turn to *do something* for the group, to guess the action and to chant the transformation.
3. Action Game with Objects—Verb to Noun Phrase
   a. Repeat action game in Step 1.
   b. Ask child who is doing something, "What else can you do at the same time?" If necessary, offer suggestions, such as, "Can you walk while you eat?"
   c. Start a new chant to incorporate both actions in verbs, such as, "He is walking and eating."

d. Change the chant to transform to a noun phrase, such as, "He is a walking eater."

e. Elicit other actions for an "eater" from other children. "What else can you do while you're eating?" "Johnny was a skipping eater."

f. Continue to lead the transformation until some children show they can make such transformations.

g. Other transformations children may suggest:

VERB FORM	NOUN FORM	NOUN PHRASE
eating	eater	walking eater talking eater running eater skipping eater
drumming	drummer	walking drummer talking drummer marching drummer sitting drummer
singing	singer	walking singer hopping singer dancing singer clapping singer

4.18 WORD GAMES: PRACTICING PRONOUN USE
GROUP SIZE: 5, ALL

Behavioral Goals

1. Children practice producing selected standard syntactic forms.
2. Children transform nouns and noun phrases to pronouns.

Procedure

Materials

Tape recorder and microphone

1. Invite a small group of children to play the talking game, using the microphone.
2. Improvise the game to generate humor, through gross exaggeration or surprise.
3. Start with simplest task requiring transformation to first person pronoun *I*.
    a. Say, "If you are John, who is John?" Elicit response, "I am John."
    b. Say, "Sheila, if you are a lollipop, who is a lollipop?"
    c. Continue humorous questions requiring transformation to "I" form.
4. Initiate transformations to other singular and plural pronouns:
    a. Say, "If I have blue earrings, who has blue earrings?" Elicit, "You have blue earrings."
    b. Say, "If Billy had a haircut, who had a haircut?" Elicit, "He had a haircut."
    c. Say, "If Sondra is wearing red shoes, who is wearing red shoes?" Elicit, "She is wearing red shoes."
    d. Say, "If our class goes to the zoo, who goes to the zoo?" Elicit, "We go to the zoo."
    e. Say, "If the class next door goes to the museum, who goes to the museum?" Elicit, "They go to the museum."
5. Invite children to hear a replay of the tape recording, for fun and for repetitive practice for children who are interested.

Variation

Encourage children, when ready, to take teacher role.

4.19 WORD GAMES: VERBS–3RD PERSON SINGULAR
GROUP SIZE: 5, ALL

Behavioral Goals

1. Children practice producing selected standard syntactic forms.
2. Children produce third person singular forms of verbs in present tense, with *s*, in standard form.

Procedure

A. ACTION GAME

    1. Ask children to form a circle.
    2. Model the rules. Walk around the circle, touch one child and say, "If he jumps, we jump." This child becomes "it."
    3. First child, "it," walks around circle, touches another child, says, "If he hops, we hop."
    4. Encourage children to use variety of action, to practice variety of verbs.

B. SINKING AND FLOATING GAME

Materials

Glass aquarium

Variety of sinking and floating objects

    1. Model the rules. Say, "If it sinks, it's John's. If it floats, it's Mary's."
    2. Demonstrate action and verbalization.
    3. Offer objects for independent activity.

4.20 NAME RECOGNITION AND REPLICATION WITHOUT WRITING
GROUP SIZE: 1, 2, 5

Behavioral Goal

Children replicate names with precut letters and name alphabet letters.

Procedure

Materials

For each child:
Envelope

Letters of his name

Name card, first name only

Individual flannel board

A. MATCHING FLANNEL LETTERS TO NAME CARD

1. Invite one child at a time to find his name card, helping as needed.
2. Give child letters of his first name in an envelope and ask him to match these to his name card. If necessary, demonstrate with the first letter.
3. Help child check his work, comparing letter with letter, from left to right, naming letters. Refrain from testing child's knowledge of letter names by telling him if he falters.

B. SELECTING AND ORDERING FLANNEL LETTERS

Materials

Same as above, plus additional precut letters

1. Ask the child to select the envelope marked with his first name.
2. Playfully tell child, "You're too smart. I have to make this harder." Increase the challenge by adding a few letters or by hiding the name card, or in another way.

C. SELECTING AND ORDERING MAGNETIC LETTERS

Materials

Individual name cards

Magnaboard

Set of upper and lower case magnetic letters

1. Ask the child to select and order letters of his full name, using name card if needed.
2. Ask the child to check and label magnetic letters against name card.
3. Ask children to order letters of each other's names, checking and labeling against name cards.

D. REPLICATING NAMES WITH LETTER STAMPS

Materials

Upper and lower case letter stamps

Inked stamp pad

Paper

1. Have children use letter stamps playfully in any way they like.
2. Ask children to select letter stamps to replicate names, words, and sentences using name or word cards as needed.

E. INITIATE TYPING NAMES. (See Lang. 4.21.)

Further Reference

Language 4.21

4.21 USE OF PRIMER TYPEWRITER
GROUP SIZE: 1, 2

Behavioral Goals

Use the primer typewriter as an additional piece of equipment for children's practice in the following skills:

1. Naming and differentiating letters of the alphabet and numerals.
2. Differentiating and matching upper- and lower-case letters.
3. Spacing between words.
4. Replicating one's name, first and last.
5. Replicating words.
6. Constructing and replicating simple sentences.
7. Using forms of standard English syntax.
8. Composing simple stories.
9. Learning sound-symbol relationships.
10. Punctuating simple sentences.

Procedure

1. Make the typewriter available for the use of one child at a time, with adult supervision, until the child demonstrates ability to follow the rules for typewriter operation independently.
2. Keep the typewriter keyboard in locked position, except when in use.
3. Introduce names of typewriter parts as these are used. Names include key, carriage, carriage return bar, space and back space bar, shift key and shift lock for upper- and lower-case, bell, margin, and punctuation marks, such as period and comma. Introduce other terms in context such as strike, return, press, firmly, slowly, position, repeat, insert, remove, roll, down, and up.
4. Make an alphabet chart to associate the upper- and lower-case forms of each letter, as follows:

A	B	C
a	b	c

Note that the lower-case type form of some letters, such as *a* may be different from the manuscript form, and if so, both forms are needed on the chart. The chart can be taped to the typewriter, above the keyboard, where it can be accessible to the child. The chart will probably be too long for the typewriter and will probably require being folded when not in use.

5. Rules for Typewriter Operation
   a. Insert paper first.
   b. Strike one key at a time. Wait until key returns.
   c. Press space bar to make a space.
   d. When bell rings, return carriage slowly, but firmly, by pressing carriage return bar.
   e. Lock shift key to type upper-case letters.
   f. Unlock shift key to type lower-case letters.
6. Work with one child at a time. Allow other children to watch. Set wide margins and spacer for double spacing.
7. Demonstrate inserting paper, using specific typewriter labels in context.
8. Set typewriter for upper-case. Say, "We lock the shift key to type upper-case letters." Strike a key, demonstrating and verbalizing the rules. Say, "I am striking the key. Then I let go. Now look! See, that's the first letter of your name. It's an upper-case __(name the letter)." Use the term *upper-case* for capitals, without explanation. When the term *lower-case* is introduced later, differentiate between them by labeling, without explanation.
9. Ask the child to copy the demonstration.
10. Suggested initial typing practice.
    a. Ask the child to repeat striking the first key several times. Continue to name the letter as he strikes the keys.
    b. Demonstrate unlocking shift key, to type the lower-case form of the same letter. Encourage child to practice typing upper- and lower-case forms of same letter. Supervise this playfully, asking child to be alert to which one you name.
    c. Explain use of alphabet chart, described in step 4, associating upper- and lower-case forms of letters. Say, "Run your finger across the top line of this chart until you find the upper-case letter you just typed." When child fingers this letter on the chart, say, "You will find the lower-case letter right beneath it."
    d. Child may type whole first name. Demonstrate spacing between words.
    e. Child may practice typing series of upper- and lower-case letters.
    f. Child may type his whole name.
    g. Child may type friends' names.
    h. Child may type words he chooses.
    i. Child may start to type words and sentences as suggested by the beginning reading sequence, Structure Model 4.61.

11. After the child's initial introduction to the typewriter, repeat the rules, in context, in succeeding sessions until children demonstrate mastery of these rules.
12. It would be desirable to keep most of the children's typing on file at school, for children's and teacher's reference, sending home occasional samples.

4.22 MANUSCRIPT WRITING
GROUP SIZE: 2, 5

Behavioral Goals

1. Using manuscript form, children write their own names, simple words, and sentences.
2. Children apply positional terms in writing.

Procedure

Materials

For each child, prepare about 25 sheets of primer-lined paper, with the child's name written on first line.

Pencils

Crayons

Felt-tipped pens

1. Prepare a duplicator master as above, and run as many copies as needed.
2. Tape a manuscript writing chart to a wall, at children's eye level, to show shape and direction of writing strokes.
3. For each child, write a model of each letter of his name on his paper, emphasizing the direction and shape of strokes. Say, "Donald, I am writing an upper-case *D*, the first letter of your name. We write it like this: First, this straight line down to here, then this rounded line from here to here."
4. Help child, as needed, to trace the duplicated model of his name. Stress the fact that most letters are formed with strokes that are either straight lines or rounded lines. Use positional terms and descriptive terms of size, shape, and quantity.

Key Language

Top	Bottom
Left	Right
First row	Next to
Before	After
Up	Down
Below	Above

Big	Little
Long	Short
Straight	Round
Even	Double
Pair	Two

5. As children learn to write their names, encourage them to write their names on their art work or any other paper work.
6. Encourage interested children to write:
   a. Other children's names;
   b. Simple words and sentences;
   c. Labels for classroom play activities;
   d. Name cards and tasks for helper chart. See Soc. 7.11, Item 3;
   e. Anything they wish to write.

Further Reference

Sociology 7.11

4.50 MODEL DIALOGUE USING PUPPETS, TO PRACTICE NEGATION
GROUP SIZE: 5, ALL

Procedure

Materials

A green cube

A little ball

A puppet

T	Good morning. My name is Applehead. What's my name?
Ch	Applehead!
T	I thought my name was John Robinson. (laughter) Is that my name?
Ch	No!
T	That's not my name? I forgot! What is my name?
Ch	Applehead!
T	Oh, thank you. Sometimes I forget things. I'm going to show you what I learned in school. Do you want to help me?
Ch	Yes.
T	All right. Here is . . . a . . . red . . . block.
Ch	It is green!
T	Are you trying to tell me it is or it is not a red block?
Ch	It is not a red block.
T	It is not a red block?
Ch	No!
T	Oh, poor Applehead. Let me see. Here, I have a bell.
Ch	That's not a bell! It's a ball.
T	It's a bell. Watch me ring it. Ting-a-ling.
Ch	No. It is not a bell. It is a ball.
T	It is not a bell?
Ch	It's not a bell. It's a ball.
T	You're right. It's a great, big ball.
Ch	No, it's a little ball.
T	I thought that this was a big ball.
Ch	That's a little ball.
T	This is *not* a big ball?
Ch	No. It's a little ball.
T	It is a little ball. Oh, I finally got that one right. Do you want to give me a kiss? Thank you. Do you like my red dress?
Ch	It's a green dress.
T	Are you trying to tell me that my dress is or is not red?

Ch It's not red.

T It's not red? What color is it?

Ch It's green.

T It's a good thing you children know so much. Here is a fork.

Ch It's a spoon. It's a spoon.

T Oh, I think it's a fork.

Ch It's a spoon. Spoon! A red spoon. A red spoon.

T This is *not* a fork?

Ch No! It's a red spoon.

T You're right again.

T Come here little kittycat.

Ch I'm not no kittycat.

Ch She's not a kitty. This is a girl. She's a girl. (laughter)

T You're right. She's not a kitty. She's a girl. Look at that banana. Are you a banana?

Ch (much noise, shouts of) No!

T What are you? You're not a banana? And look, here's a little orange. Are you an orange?

Ch (much laughter, shouts of) No!

T Are you trying to tell me you are or you are not an orange?

Ch I'm not a' orange.

T Did you say, "I am not an orange?"

Ch Yes. I'm not an orange.

T You're not an orange. Well you look as sweet as an orange. Give me a kiss. (puppet kisses child, much laughter)

T Here is a boy who is wearing a bicycle. Can you ride on this bicycle?

Ch No.

T Are you saying that this is or that this is not a bicycle?

Ch It is not a bicycle. It's a tie.

4.60 PHONICS: SOUND-SYMBOL RELATIONSHIPS
GROUP SIZE: 2, 5

Behavioral Goals

Children associate consonant sounds with alphabet letters.

Procedure

1. Tape upper- and lower-case letter names to outside of object box. Separate the two forms for clarity.
2. Invite two children to work with the object box, on an initial consonant sound.
3. Work with object boxes.

Materials

Object boxes with attractive materials which represent words with initial consonant sounds of b, d, f, h, l, m, n, p, r, t, v, and w.

Initial consonant sounds for c, g, j, k, q, and s are less regular and are introduced much later.

Examples:[1]

B-b	bat	F-f	fur
	ball		felt
	boat		fish
	basket		feather
D-d	dog	H-h	hat
	disc		hanger
	dinosaur		horn
	domino		hatchet
L-l	lock	R-r	rock
	lamp		ring
	leaf		rat
	lid		rabbit
M-m	match	T-t	tank
	mat		tie
	mask		tape
	marble		telephone

[1] Avoid initial consonant blends, such as *br*ick. In each word used, the initial consonant is followed by a vowel.

N-n	net	V-v	vest
	needle		vase
	nail		veil
	napkin		velvet
P-p	pear	W-w	wagon
	pig		wire
	pants		wood
	pearl		watch

a. Label each item in the box, exaggerating the initial sound, encouraging the children to handle the objects and repeat the names.

b. Say, "This is our B-box. All these things begin with the 'buh' sound. Can you see other things in this room that begin with the same sound?" Help children by pointing out some objects, if they do not identify them.

c. Say, "Each of you go get one thing that we can add to our B-box." Help children, if necessary.

d. Follow this procedure for the initial consonants listed above.

4. Mystery Bag Game

Materials

Bag

Assorted objects representing initial consonants listed above

Object boxes

a. Place selected objects in a bag.

b. Tell child to select one object box, and to sound out its initial letter.

c. Ask child to sort out from the mystery bag those objects that belong in his box.

d. Change objects often, to keep interest high.

e. Vary the responsibility for filling the mystery bag by assigning specified children to add items either from the classroom or from home.

5.   Letter Books

Materials

Construction paper

Paste

Crayons

Scissors

Picture magazines

Duplicated picture sheets and objects supplied by teacher and children

a.   Invite a child to make a letter book for one initial consonant sound.
b.   Let child select from such alternatives as drawing a picture, cutting out pictures or pasting objects.

4.61 BEGINNING READING: ADAPTED LINGUISTIC METHOD[1]

An adaptation of the *Merrill Linguistic Readers* is proposed as a specific, sequenced plan to initiate young children into the process of decoding words and simple sentences. Phonics practice, detailed in Lang. 4.60, is expected to be initiated prior to beginning reading instruction, and to continue along with the child's decoding practice.

Although prototype teaching sequences are specified, teachers are expected to use these proposals with judgment and flexibility, adapting them to the developing needs and interests of each child. The specific teaching procedures listed are to be viewed as proposed guides for teachers who interact daily with the children they teach. Teachers are not expected to thrust reading instruction upon unwilling children. In the same spirit as all the other aspects of this curriculum design, teachers are expected to help children to experience broadened horizons, new ideas and new interests and to work with those individual children who are willing to practice new skills.

It is intended that beginning reading instruction be informal, tutorial, and voluntary. Individualization, flexibility, and adaptation to the child are featured throughout this program in beginning reading instruction, as well as in other content areas.

Entering Behavior Required

1. Attention span requisite to the task.
2. Moderate ability to produce and respond to some common forms of standard English speech.
3. Child's willingness and interest in the task.
4. Ability to identify and name all alphabet letters—upper- and lower-case.

Note: Some children with high interest in reading tasks may be permitted to start initial reading instruction before mastery of letter recognition, since this reading method features alphabet learning.

5. Content of reading program:
   a. See *Reader I, Merrill Linguistic Readers, Teacher's Edition*, for suggested word lists.
   b. All of the sets of words in the initial series belong to a major set of spelling patterns composed of three-letter words, in which the vowels are followed by the same consonant but preceded by various consonants of minimum contrast. Examples are *cap, lap, tap*.
   c. A few high frequency sight words are also used, which are not in the

[1] This method is adapted from the linguistic method specified in Fries, W. and Fries, R. 1966. *Merrill Linguistic Readers, A Basic Program of Six Books for the Primary Grades*, Columbus, Ohio, Charles E. Merrill Publishing Company. See *Teacher's Guide for Reader I*.

regular spelling patterns featured. Sight words include: *is*, *a*, *the*, *on*, *not*, *look*, *to*, *be*, and *I*. The sight words are not spelled, but are to be taught as configurational patterns.

d. The selected words for children's replication and decoding are supplemented by individual word card collections, or sentences, which the teacher writes upon the child's request. This collection is developed by eliciting from the child any words he especially wishes to type or to replicate. Each child's word collection can be kept in an envelope, with his name on the outside, for his voluntary use.

e. An individual story booklet may be typed by a child who wishes to construct a story. The teacher offers help, as needed, and encourages the child to read his story to other children and to take it home to read to his family.

Procedure

1. Work with one child at a time.
2. Identify the children who meet the entering behavior requirements. Check children's alphabet mastery by a simple test of their ability to identify upper- and lower-case letters presented randomly.
3. The suggested linguistic approach to decoding, as adapted here, follows this sequence:
   a. Confine beginning reading instruction to selected short words with regular, predictable sound-symbol relationships.
   b. Help children learn to distinguish the spelling patterns of two words with minimum contrast, such as cat-fat, by pronouncing and replicating them. Replicate with felt, hardboard, sandpaper or magnetic letters, by letter stamps, handwriting, or typewriting. The preferred method is by typewriting on a primer typewriter, or one with large type.
   c. Add a few sight words so that simple sentences may be constructed for replication.
4. Writing is integrated with reading skills, whenever possible. See Lang. 4.22.
5. Supplementary reading materials are to be introduced from time to time. Such reading material may consist of:
   a. Stories teachers read to children, especially the Dr. Seuss type *I Can Read* books.
   b. Stories developed from meaningful class experiences, of very brief sentences, and self-evident meanings, using photographs or other illustrations. See Lang. 4.60.
   c. Any trade book the child selects which he finds within his reading skills.

Further Reference

Language 4.60

4.62 SAMPLE INITIAL DECODING INSTRUCTION
GROUP SIZE: 1

Procedure

Materials

Any of the following:

Flannel letters on flannel board

Magnetic letters on magnetic board

Primer-typed letters on cards, one letter to a card

Similar materials

1. Prepare 2 words: *cat, fat*.
2. Pronounce 1 word, then spell the word, pointing to the individual letters.
3. Use the word in a sentence.
4. Repeat steps 2 and 3 for second word.
5. Help the child to type the words, to say them, and to spell them as he types.
6. Ask child to show how the 2 words differ. If the child cannot show how the 2 words differ:
   a. Line up the 2 words, 1 above the other.
   b. Compare the letters of the 2 words, from left to right. If cat and fat are the words to be compared, then the words are aligned thus:

   c a t
   f a t

   Ask the child to point to the first letter in each word, to name the letters and to say whether these are the same, and then to compare the other two letters. If the child is unable to make letter distinctions, in words, he needs more practice with alphabet letters.
7. Ask child to practice duplicating the words, by typing them or otherwise.
8. Repeat steps 2 through 7 for additional pairs of words, then with word families. See word lists in *Reader I, Merrill Linguistic Readers, Teacher's Edition*, for instructional sequence.

CHART A: WORD LIST FOR TEACHER REFERENCE[1]

Words in Pattern	Sight Words	Words in Pattern	Sight Words
cat fat Nat	is a	map nap tap	
pat	the	Dad Dad's had bad	he
mat sat	on	Nat's	
hat	not	mad sad	
rat bat at	look	bag rag tag	
can man ran Dan		bats pats	and
fan pan van	to	taps maps	
		bags rags tags	
cap lap		wag wags rags	I
Dan's		am	

[1]Fries, W. and Fries, R. 1966. *Reader I, Merrill Linguistic Readers, Teacher's Edition*, reprinted by permission of Charles E. Merrill Publishing Company, Columbus, Ohio.

4.63 SAMPLE INITIAL SIGHT WORD INSTRUCTION
GROUP SIZE: 1

Procedure

Materials

    Select from the following:

        Flannel letters on flannel board

        Magnetic letters on magnetic board

        Primer-typed letters on cards, one letter to a card

1. Introduce new sight words, *is* and *a*, by assembling the letters and pronouncing (but *not* spelling) them.
2. Use the new sight words in sentences with the words already learned, such as *cat-fat*.
3. Give the child the model sentence, "A cat is fat," either handwritten or in precut letters, and ask him to type it.
4. When the child types the sentence correctly, ask him to read it.
5. Children who wish to, and are able, may practice writing the new words and sentences on inch-ruled paper, copying a model written by the teacher. See Lang. 4.22 for writing instruction.
6. Continue to invite children to copy sentences using new sight words, as they are introduced.
7. Invite children to construct sentences as their reading vocabulary expands.

Further Reference

Language 4.22

4.64 MAKING AND READING BOOKLETS
GROUP SIZE: 1, 5, ALL

Behavioral Goals

1. Children narrate stories they have heard.
2. Children dictate simple sentences and narratives about observations and experiences.
3. Children use precise name labels and descriptive terms.
4. Children use full sentences of standard English forms.
5. Children recognize their names when they see them.
6. Children enjoy listening to stories.
7. Children read simple sentences.

Procedure

Materials

Paper

Construction paper for covers

Paste

Crayons

Pencils

Decorative materials

A. DUPLICATED BOOKLETS

1. Initiate this activity after an exciting class activity such as a shopping trip, or making fresh orange juice or pancakes, or a carpentry project.
2. Conduct a brief discussion with group to construct a story about the experience. Elicit details from children and suggestions for the story.
3. Compose a short simple story of about four sentences, one sentence to a page. Draw very simple illustrations which the children have the option to color, or let the children make their own illustrations.
4. Invite children to make a construction paper cover for their own booklets, decorating by crayoning or pasting. Ask children to write their names helping them if necessary.
5. Read the book several times with small groups.
6. Give each child his booklet to take home to read to his family.
7. Place several booklets in class library for children to read.

B. INDIVIDUALLY DICTATED SENTENCES AND STORIES

1. Work with a child who is excited about a recent experience or who responds with enthusiasm to his own painting or to the stimulation of questions or comments.

2. Invite child to dictate a sentence or two about his interest. Handwrite or type on the lower half of a sheet of construction paper. Write his name on paper and offer him the opportunity to illustrate the page if he wishes.

4.80 RHYMING WORDS AND NONSENSE SYLLABLES
GROUP SIZE: 5

Behavioral Goals

Children recognize rhymes, produce simple and nonsense rhymes, and practice rhyming.

Procedure

Materials

   Nursery rhymes or folk rhymes with which children are familiar[1]

A. LEARNING RHYMES AND SUBSTITUTING RHYMES

1. Recite the rhyme clearly and rhythmically, inviting the children to recite it with you.
2. Suggest appropriate action or invite children to suggest action, to accompany the rhyme. For example, if the rhyme is "One, Two, Buckle My Shoe," the action may be pretending to buckle one's shoe.
3. Select a series of rhymes for children to learn, so that they soon have a repertoire of learned rhymes.
4. After children have learned a series of rhymes, ask children to make up rhymes, to add to the ones they have learned. For example, with the rhyme "One, Two, Buckle My Shoe," say, "I can think of a different rhyme for 'One, two, buckle my shoe.' I can say, 'One, two, who are you?' What can you say?"
5. Offer rhyme examples freely until children begin to catch on to the "rhyming" quality.
6. Accept nonsense rhymes as well as word rhymes, since they both reflect understanding of the concept of *rhyme*.

B. PRACTICING RHYMING

Materials

   Boxes of miniature objects

1. Select small objects with names that rhyme, such as cat-bat or sock-rock.
2. Ask children to take object out of the box and help them label the objects.

---

[1] Folk rhymes refer to the ditties children chant to jump rope or bounce balls, such as "Down the Mississippi ____."

3. Say, "Let's play a game. Derrick will pick out an object and tell me its name, and I will find an object with a rhyming name. Then someone else will pick out an object." Demonstrate rhyming by matching the object with one which has a rhyming name.
4. Continue to demonstrate rhyming until each child has had several turns to select object.
5. Gradually, invite children to help you find an object with a rhyming name.
6. As the children learn the rhyming pairs, change your role and select the first object. Ask a child to match a rhyming name.
7. Later, change the objects selected for rhyming practice, to introduce new rhymes.
8. Later, use pictures along with the objects.
9. Later, use pictures without the objects.

Independent Activities

1. Invite children to play the game without you.
2. Invite children to clip pictures from magazines and paste rhyming pairs in a booklet. Write the word names on the page in manuscript or invite the child to write or use letter stamps.

More Examples of Folk Rhymes

1. Rain, rain, go away.
    Come again another day
    Little Johnny wants to play.
2. It's raining, it's pouring,
    The old man is snoring.
    He got into bed,
    And bumped his head,
    And couldn't get up in the morning.
3. Snow, snow faster.
    Ally, ally, blaster.
    The old woman's baking a pie.
    She'll let me eat some bye and bye.
4. A knife and a fork.
    A bottle and a cork.
    That's the way
    to spell *New York*.
5. I'm rubber and you're glue.
    What you say to me will bounce back and stick to you.

Further Reference

1. Withers, C. 1948. *A Rocket in My Pocket, The Rhymes and Chants of Young Americans*, N. Y., Holt & Co.
2. Opie, C. and Opie. P. 1951. *The Oxford Dictionary of Nursery Rhymes*, Oxford, The Claredon Press.
3. Evans, P. 1961. *Rimbles*, N. Y., Doubleday.

4.90 CREATIVE DRAMATIZATION
GROUP SIZE: 5, ALL

Behavioral Goals

1. Children dramatize and narrate familiar stories or recent experiences.
2. Children dramatize events in sequence.

Procedure

Materials

Simple props for dramatization, such as:

Scarf

A teacher-made "animal face," consisting of a paper headband and two long "ears"

1. Help children recall the sequence of the story to be dramatized.
2. Help children identify the characters and specify the action.
3. Cast roles either by assignment or by volunteers.
4. Direct a practice session by narrating or otherwise helping children to act the story. Encourage children to use their own words and to develop their own actions. Avoid memorization.
5. Refrain from correcting children's speech or actions. Gradually, help children recall more details about the role or provide further sources of information, such as reading them a story or arranging a trip to note further detail.
6. Decrease your leadership role as children grow more skillful in dramatizations.
7. Multiply roles to include as many children as possible in the dramatization. For example, in store play, there can be many customers; in "Caps for Sale," there can be any number of monkeys; in "Ask Mr. Bear," there can be any number of animals.

Further Reference

Sociology 7.20

Mathematics

5.00   Goals in Mathematics
5.01   Materials List
5.10   One-to-One Matching
5.11   Sets: Members, Nonmembers and Subsets; Pick-Up Game, Magnet Hunt, Eureka Game
5.12   Copying Model Sets: Copy Cat Game, Chart A
5.13   Making Equivalent Sets: Chart B
5.20   Geometric Shapes
5.30   Identifying Grossly Unequal Sets as Having More or Less: Happy Clown Game, Chart C
5.31   Sets: More, Less, the Same Number; Coffee Can Game
5.32   Sets: Use of Symbols for More, Less and the Same Number; Draw-a-Card Game
5.42   Counting Objects
5.44   Meanings of Zero
5.45   Tallies and Graphs
5.50   Numerals
5.51   Writing Numerals
5.52   Ordinal Sequence
5.53   One-More Game
5.60   Ordering Objects by Length: Mr. Long Game
5.70   Arbitrary Linear Measurement
5.71   Standard Linear Measurement
5.72   Some Standard Measures for Liquids
5.80   Combining Sets up to a Total of 10
5.81   Addition Using Symbols: Get Rich Game
5.82   Subtraction Using Symbols: Lucky Beans
5.90   Conservation of Number: Chart D

5.00 GOALS IN MATHEMATICS

Beginning mathematics involves number, shape, measurement, operations, and number vocabulary. The abstract concept of number is developed through experiences with sets of objects. Each child builds his own understandings of number from his manipulation and experiences with things. The dilemma of when to pose a problem or when to offer information can only be resolved by the teacher in each instance. An informal methodology is followed, which includes games, puzzles, structured teaching episodes and problem-solving activities, in addition to playful manipulation.

Behavioral Goals

A. NUMBERS AND NUMERATION
1. Sets
    a. Children match a set of objects one-to-one to another set of objects.
    b. Children differentiate members of sets from nonmembers of sets.
    c. Children sort objects into specified sets.
    d. Children make a copy of a set of objects.
    e. Children determine whether a set has more, less, or the same number of objects as another set.
    f. Children conserve number when objects in set are rearranged, or replacements are made.
2. Number and Operations
    a. Children associate a given number with sets of that size.
    b. Children associate numerals with the number of objects in a set.
    c. Children use zero to represent an empty set.
    d. Children write numerals.
    e. Children join two sets of objects and apply a number to the newly created set.
    f. Children order numbers by the relation of *one more*.
    g. Children arrange sets in the ordinal sequence.
    h. Children partition sets into two groups and identify the number of objects in each subset.
    i. Children develop number recording methods including tallying and graphing.

B. GEOMETRIC CONCEPTS

1. Children differentiate and name solid geometric shapes and identify them as spheres or balls, cubes, cones, rectangular solids, or cylinders.
2. Children identify and label figures as rectangles, squares, triangles, or circles.
3. Children reproduce geometric figures with materials such as crayon and string.

C. MEASUREMENT

1. Children differentiate and label gross differences in measurement, as longer-shorter, bigger-smaller, heavier-lighter.
2. Children order groups of three or more objects on differences in lengths.
3. Children use arbitrary measures.
4. Children use and identify units of standard measures of liquids and length.

5.01 MATERIALS LIST

For a classroom to provide enough experience, a wide variety of materials should be available for the children to play with, to sort, to arrange in patterns, and later to count. Most of these materials are inexpensive and many can be collected by the children themselves. Coffee cans with plastic lids, cigar boxes, and tea and cookie tins make excellent storage containers and are sturdy enough for classroom use. In addition, covering the top of a cigar box makes an excellent individual flannel board.

1. Identical materials (any item can be substituted for any other item)

Kidney beans	Paper cups
Paper clips	Dry macaroni
Milk cartons	Napkins
Tongue depressors	Tissues
Cookies	Plastic bottles
Spring clothespins	Raisins
Rubber bands	Dry cereals

2. Similar materials (vary only by color)

New crayons	Pegs
Checkers	Pipe cleaners
Poker chips	Multicolored toothpicks
Shoe laces	Straws
Counting cubes	Beads
Buttons	

3. Related materials (classes of things)

Paper flowers	Buttons
Miniature cars and trucks	Shells
Miniature animals	Hardboard geometric shapes
Plastic bottle caps	Property blocks
Colored yarns and threads	Color cubes
Plastic forks and spoons	Felt shapes

Wooden-beads—various colors, shapes, and sizes

Unit blocks

Cards with pictures pasted and drawn on

Miniature fruits and vegetables

Balls: ping, pong, rubber, styrofoam, golf

4. Sorting materials
    Hoops or loops, using:
    Shoelaces

    Ribbon

    Rope

    Plastic-covered wire

    Ordinary string

    Paper plates, trays, or pieces of construction paper, muffin tins, plastic cutlery trays, or boxes

5. Measurement Materials
    Rulers

    Tape measures

    Yardsticks

    Measuring cups, ½ and whole cup

    Quart measures

    Teacher-made cardboard lengths

    Food coloring

    Funnels

    Measured containers

6. Additional Materials

    Magnets

    Magnetic objects

    Teacher-made number cards

    Teacher-made numeral cards

    Spinners

    Foam rubber cubes

    Symbol cards

    Numeral stamps

    Precut numerals

    Chalk and chalkboard

    Dice

    Paper cups

Further Reference
Sociology 7.20 through 7.22

5.10 ONE-TO-ONE MATCHING
GROUP SIZE: 5, ALL

Behavioral Goals

1. Children pair off as partners.
2. Children match one object to one person, such as cup, napkin, cookie.

Procedure

Materials

Items required for the activity in process, as snack, art, music, or craft project

1. Partners for activities such as dancing, taking a walk, going on a trip.
    a. Demonstrate by choosing one boy as your partner and saying, "John is my partner. I am John's partner."
    b. After all children have partners, check, "Does each boy have a girl partner? Does each girl have a boy as a partner?"
2. Distribution of Materials

Materials

Those needed for snack or other activity

1. Ask one child to distribute napkins at each table: "Give one napkin to each child at this table."
2. As child finishes, ask him to check: "See if every child has a napkin, including yourself. Go around and ask each child to show you his napkin."
3. Suggest children match objects to children, one-to-one, in such activities as distribution of art materials or musical instruments. For use with numerals, see Math. 5.42.

Further Reference

Mathematics 5.42

**5.11 SETS: MEMBERS, NONMEMBERS AND SUBSETS; PICK-UP GAME,
MAGNET HUNT, EUREKA GAME
GROUP SIZE: 5**

Behavioral Goals

1. Children differentiate members of sets from nonmembers of sets using
   Pick-up Game and Magnet Hunt.
2. Children sort objects into subsets using Eureka Game.

Key Language

Eureka	Check
Inside	Different
Set	Left over
Same	Color names
Not the same	Descriptive terms

Procedure

A. PICK-UP GAME (follows children's free exploration with magnets)

Materials

Magnet

Paper plates

Hoop or loop

3 sets of nonmagnetic objects:
  8 black checkers

  10 kidney beans

  6 green pegs

1 set of magnetic objects:
  10 paper clips

1. Allow children ample time for free exploration with magnets.
2. Scramble the 4 sets on a large paper plate.
3. Place a loop near the plate.
4. Put your hand inside the loop. Say, "Inside the loop you put the things
   the magnet can pick up."
5. Give one child the magnet. Ask him to play the game.

6. After first child finishes, give magnet to another child. Say, "Let's check to see if the magnet will pick up anything else on the plate."
7. Point to inside of loop and ask, "Are all the things in this set the same?" Verify the answer by naming the objects.
8. Ask, "What things are left on the plate?" Help children name objects if necessary.
9. Point to the plate. Say, "Are all these things the same? No, they are not the same. They are different."
10. Scramble all materials on plate. Give each child a turn to use the magnet.
11. Variation: Change the materials each time. Use only one kind of magnetic object, such as nails or thumb tacks. See Cog. Skills 2.10 and Sci. 6.11.

B. MAGNET HUNT

Materials

2 containers

Magnet

Loop

Any other objects in the room

1. Have children play independently, collecting in one container a set of objects that the magnet has picked up and in the other container a set that the magnet has not picked up.
2. When the hunt is finished, ask children to check the items in each container by using the magnet, and place all magnetic items inside the loop.

C. EUREKA GAME (sorting sets into subsets)

Materials

Tray

4 hoops

4 colors of counting cubes

Place 4 hoops on floor or on table top. Put the counting cubes on a tray and say, "Watch what I do. As soon as you can do it too, say 'Eureka' and help me." Slowly place cubes inside loops by color. If a child makes an error, ignore it. If another child corrects the error, accept it without comment. When all cubes are sorted, ask group if they need to make any changes, checking first sets without error. Ask, "What did we put in this loop?" If necessary, say, "We put yellow cubes here."

Variations on Eureka Game

1. Change the game by using different materials, but continue to sort by color.

Materials

Tray

Set of objects in 3 or 4 different colors, such as:
½-inch wooden beads

Same number of hoops as colors

2. Change the game from sorting by color to sorting by length (short-long).

Materials

Tray

2 hoops

Set of colored pipe cleaners or straws, some cut in half

3. Change game to sorting by such other properties as hard-soft or light-heavy.

Materials

Tray

2 hoops

Sets of contrasting materials such as:
Unit blocks

Foam rubber blocks or sponges

Ping pong and golf balls

4. Change game to sorting by shape, size or thickness, changing number of hoops as needed, with the same materials. It is very difficult for young children to change the base for sorting. Be playful, use cues, and expect that some children's progress will be slow.

Materials

Tray

Hoops

Property blocks

5. Sort miniature objects by class, for example, tools or eating utensils, fruits, or vegetables.

Materials

Tray

Hoops

Miniature objects

D. SORTING IN CRAFT ACTIVITIES

1. Ask child to select a set of decorative materials for a single purpose collage, book, or mobile. Examples: a triangle collage, an all blue design, a sequin design on a pencil holder. See Soc. 7.20, 7.21.

Further Reference

Cognitive Skills 2.10
Science 6.11
Sociology 7.20, 7.21

5.12 COPYING MODEL SETS
GROUP SIZE: 1, 2, 5

Behavioral Goals

1. Children select objects to copy a model set.
2. Children make equivalent sets.
3. Children verbalize *same* and *not the same* or *different*.

Procedure

A. COPY CAT GAME (Chart A, *1a*)

Materials

Box or tray containing 8 pairs of objects and 2 pieces of construction paper on which objects will be placed. See Chart A, *1a*.

1. Invite child to play. Say, "Let's play a game. See if you can be a copy cat. Here is my paper and here's your paper."
2. Select 5 different objects from the box, placing them on your paper in a row. Say, "This is my set of objects. Be a copy cat and make a set on your paper that is just like mine."
3. Use checking procedures as follows:
    a. Leave each set on its own paper.
    b. Slide the two pieces of paper next to each other.
    c. Say, "Let's check. I have a cow." Move the cow to the edge of the paper.
    d. Say, "Where is your cow?" Point to the position on child's paper where he is to place his cow.
    e. Check remaining objects in the same way. Maintain as brisk a pace as possible. When checked, the two sets look like this:

cow	0	0	cow
truck	0	0	truck
crayon	0	0	crayon
fork	0	0	fork
cup	0	0	cup

B. VARIATIONS OF COPY CAT GAME (Chart A, 1*b*, 2*a*, 2*b*)

1. Repeat Copy Cat Game with different sets of objects.
2. Reverse roles with child. Child becomes the leader, creates the model set, and leads the checking procedure.
3. Reverse roles and make errors for child to correct.
4. Children make sets for each other to copy.
5. Vary the sets using different materials and more than one of a kind. Increase the number of objects in a set.

C. EVALUATION

Check children's mastery of copying model sets by bunching objects listed in Items 2*a* or 2*b* of Chart A. Children who show mastery move to Item 4 of Chart A, and match color *and* number of objects.

CHART A: COPYING MODEL SETS

Teacher Prepares	Teacher Presents Model Set A	Child Constructs Matching Set B	Task
1. a box or tray containing 8 pairs of objects	a. 1 cow, 1 truck, 1 crayon, 1 fork, and 1 cup *in a row*	same as Set A	identical copy of mixed objects— 1 each of 5 objects
2 pieces of construction paper	b. vary objects and size of sets	same as Set A	
2. two boxes, each containing no more than 12 objects, such as 3 cows, 3 forks, 2 trucks, 4 red pegs	a. 2 cows, 1 truck, 1 crayon, 2 forks, and 1 cup, or similar mixture *in a row*	same as Set A	identical copy of mixed objects— with 1 or more of a kind
2 pieces of construction paper	b. vary objects and size of sets—*in a row*	same as Set A	
3. evaluation: repeat Item 2, *bunching objects*	same as Item 2—*bunch objects*	same as Item 2	same as item 2
4. two boxes, each containing 5 each of 4 colors of cubes	2 red, 3 yellow, 3 green colored cubes, *row or bunch*	same as Set A	identical copy of similar objects, more than 1 of each
2 pieces of construction paper			

5.13 MAKING EQUIVALENT SETS
GROUP SIZE: 1

Behavioral Goals

1. Children match a set of objects to a given set of objects.
2. Children disregard all properties of sets except the number property.

Procedure

Smarty Cat Game

Materials

Described in Chart B

1. Make a model set of animals inside a loop. Ask the child to make a set of macaroni in his loop so that there are as many items as in your loop. Say, "It's feeding time. Will you put in your loop one piece of macaroni for each of my animals?"
2. For checking procedure tell child to feed animals by placing one piece of macaroni next to each animal. Encourage child to make any corrections needed, either to discard surplus macaroni or to add additional pieces.

Variations on Smarty Cat Game

1. Using Chart B, 1b, repeat Smarty Cat Game, varying the objects and size of sets.
2. Using Chart B, 2, repeat game, making model set a set of identical objects, to which child matches a different set of identical objects.
3. Using Chart B, 3, repeat game, introducing color variable, which child has to ignore.
4. Evaluation: Check children's mastery of making equivalent sets, ignoring color, as in Chart B, 3. Children who show mastery move to Chart B, 5, matching object to object, ignoring all properties but number and Chart B, 6, matching one-to-one.

Mathematics 5.13

CHART B: MAKING EQUIVALENT SETS

Teacher's Box	Child's Box	Model—Set A	Copy—Set B	Task
1. 10 to 15 related objects, such as farm animals 1 loop	10 to 15 identical objects, such as macaroni shells 1 loop	a. 7 farm animals b. vary objects and size of sets	7 macaroni shells equivalent set of macaroni shells	matching identical objects to non-identical objects
2. 10 identical objects, such as red poker chips 1 loop	10 identical objects, different from those in T box, such as blue straws 1 loop	8 red poker chips	8 blue straws	matching identical objects to a different set of identical objects
3. poker chips, 6 each of red, white, and blue 1 loop	colored cubes, 6 each of green, yellow, orange 1 loop	4 red, 3 white, 2 blue poker chips	9 cubes, any color	matching object to object, ignoring color
4. evaluation: determine mastery of task 3 before proceeding				
5. mixture of 10 objects 1 loop	mixture of 10 objects all different from T set 1 loop	variety of objects, e.g., poker chips, unit blocks, toothpicks and crayons	variety of objects (different from Set A) e.g., paper cups, straws, paper clips, rubber bands	matching object to object, ignoring all properties
6. 12 black checkers 1 loop	12 black checkers 1 loop	9 bunched black checkers	9 black checkers	matching one-to-one

5.20 GEOMETRIC SHAPES
GROUP SIZE: 1, 2, 5

Behavioral Goals

1. Children construct and name solid geometric shapes, such as spheres or balls, cubes, cones, rectangular solids, and cylinders.
2. Children construct, name, and identify flat geometric shapes such as circles, squares, rectangles, and triangles.

Procedure

Materials

Assorted craft materials:

Yarn

String

Construction paper

Pipe cleaners

Gummed shapes

1. In craft activities, liberally offer verbal labels of geometric shapes in context.
2. Invite several children to make a shape collage, a ball mobile, or a triangle book.
3. Elicit descriptions and labels of shapes used and created by children.

Further Reference

Sociology 7.20-7.22

5.30 IDENTIFYING GROSSLY UNEQUAL SETS AS HAVING MORE OR LESS: HAPPY CLOWN GAME
GROUP SIZE: 2

Behavioral Goal

Children compare two unequal sets of objects for *more* or *less*.

<u>*Procedure*</u>

Materials

15 identical objects, such as beans or macaroni

2 paper cups

1 box with picture of a happy clown on lid, with a cut-out mouth

1 box with a picture of a sad clown on lid, with a cut-out mouth

1. Introduce task: "Here is the happy clown. He always gets more to eat than the sad clown."
2. Make two piles of beans, grossly unequal. Cover each pile with a paper cup. Ask children to cover their eyes. Move the cups about on the table.
3. Ask each child to choose a cup.
4. Say, "Who will feed the happy clown? Remember he always gets more to eat." When a child responds, ask, "Why?"
5. Say, "Who will feed the sad clown? Remember he always gets less."
6. After children "feed" the clowns remove box lids and say, "Which one was the happy clown? How can you tell? Which one was the sad clown? How can you tell?" Assist verbalization as needed.

CHART C: SETS: MORE, LESS, AND EQUIVALENT
(SETS NO LARGER THAN 10)

Activity	Goals	Level of Complexity	Materials
5.30 Happy Clown Game	verbal *more, less*	gross inequality in sets	2 sets, example: kidney beans, same objects in both sets 2 boxes, 1 with happy clown face, 1 with sad clown face 2 cups
5.31 Coffee Can Game	verbal *more, less,* and *same number* Estimating *more, less same number* checking one-to-one	a. gross inequality in sets b. small numerical difference between sets c. equivalent sets d. variations: size of set and materials	a. 2 sets, example: red checkers in first can, black checkers in second can 2 cans with lids 1 spring clothespin b. Same as a c. Same as a d. Miniature animals, beans, toothpicks, blocks
5.32 Draw-a-Card Game	read letter and numeral symbols identify a set as having more, less, or the same number as the model set	a. interpret letter symbols for *more, less, same number* use symbol to select set from a group of sets b. use circles instead of objects	a. model set of 5 objects such as red counting cubes 6 to 10 sets of objects on paper plates (some sets have same number of objects as model set) deck of symbol[1] cards: 6 red cards marked *M* 6 green cards marked *L* 6 yellow cards marked *S* b. one deck of symbol cards, as in a

CHART C: *(continued)*

Activity	Goals	Level of Complexity	Materials
			6 to 10 paper plates on which circles are randomly pasted
			1 model set on a paper plate such as 5 poker chips
		c. use numerals instead of circles or objects	c. deck of symbol cards as in a
			6 to 10 paper plates, on which a numeral is pasted or written
			A model paper plate with the numeral "4," and 4 poker chips

[1]*M* = more
L = less
S = same number

5.31 SETS: MORE, LESS, THE SAME NUMBER: COFFEE CAN GAME
GROUP SIZE: 2

Behavioral Goal

Children determine whether a set has *more, less* or *the same number* of objects as another set.

Procedure

A. GROSSLY UNEQUAL SETS

Materials

2 sets of objects, varying only as to color, such as red and black checkers

1. Tell children to cover their eyes. Put 3 red checkers in one can and 8 black checkers in the other. Place lid on cans.
2. Ask the children, "Which can has more objects? Which can has less objects? You cannot open the can. How else can you find out?" Encourage children to manipulate the cans.
3. Ask, "Which can has more objects? Which can has less objects?" After children respond, say, "Here's a way to check. Here's the can you say has more objects. I'll mark it with this clothespin."
4. Assign the cans and initiate the one-to-one checking procedure.
   a. Say, "Each of you take out one checker and put it on the table. Now, take out another checker."
   b. Repeat this step until one child notes he has no more. Say to this child, "Your can is empty. You have none left."
   c. To the other child, say, "You have some left over. Is that the can with the clothespin? Your can has more."

B. SMALL NUMERICAL DIFFERENCE BETWEEN SETS

Materials

Same as A

1. Place 4 red checkers on one coffee can and 5 in the other.
2. Proceed as in A.

C. EQUIVALENT SETS

Materials

Same as A

1. Put 6 red checkers in one coffee can and 6 black checkers in the other.
2. Proceed as in A. Change verbalization to, "There are no checkers left over in this can, and no checkers left over in that can. Both cans had the same number of checkers."

Variations

Vary size of sets. Vary materials. Give children leadership of game.

5.32 SETS: USE OF SYMBOLS FOR MORE, LESS AND THE SAME NUMBER; DRAW-A-CARD GAME
GROUP SIZE: 1, 2

Behavioral Goal

Children use symbols to identify a set of objects as having more, less, or the same number as a model set.

Procedure

A. THINGS

Materials

Model set of 5 objects on paper plate, such as 5 red counting cubes

6 to 10 additional sets of objects on paper plates, such as:

3 blue cars

5 pink beads

7 miniature dogs

Deck of symbol cards including:

6 red cards marked *M*

6 green cards marked *L*

6 yellow cards marked *S*

1. Give child a model plate, which is a different color from the other plates, so that he keeps track of the model plate.
2. Give child deck of mixed cards face down.
3. Tell child to draw a card, turn it over and read the symbol.
4. Tell child, "If the symbol is *M*, put the card on a plate that has more objects than the model set. If the symbol is *L*, put the card on a plate that has less objects than the model set. If the symbol is *S*, put it on the plate that has the same number of objects as the model set. Tell me when you finish."
5. Let child decide whether to discard the extra cards or to put more than 1 card on a plate or to leave some plates without cards.
6. Help child to check by one-to-one matching with model set.

B. SPOTS

Materials

Deck of cards as in 1

6 to 10 paper plates on which circles are randomly pasted

Model set: paper plate with 5 poker chips

Proceed as in A, except for the checking procedure. Tell child to check by placing each poker chip in the model set on a gummed circle on the plate he is checking.

C. NUMERALS

Materials

Deck of cards as in 1

6 to 10 paper plates each with one numeral written on it

Model set: paper plate with the numeral 4 and 4 poker chips on it

Set of loose beans

Proceed as in A, except for the checking procedure. Say, "Read the number on the plate and put that number of beans on it. Match these beans to the poker chips in the model set, to see which set has more objects."

5.42 COUNTING OBJECTS
GROUP SIZE: 2, 5

Behavioral Goals

1. Children learn number names and associate numbers with sets of objects.
2. Children create a set of objects to match a given number.

Procedure

A. COUNTING GAME

Materials

A spinner or a 2-inch foam rubber cube

One paper cup for each player

One box of about 30 beads

A playing board

1. Make a die out of foam cube, by marking 1, 2, or 3 spots on a side; or prepare a spinner with 1, 2, or 3 spots in a quadrant.
2. Tell players to take turns, spin the spinner, count the number of spots and take that number of beads out of the box, to put into their paper cups. Help the children, if necessary.
3. Tell children when the box of beads is empty, the game is over and they can start all over again.

B. LADDER GAME

Materials

Spinner or one die

Two counting cubes of different colors as markers

Playing board

1. Ask children to decide which color cube they want as their marker.
2. Have children take turns with the spinner, count the number of dots and, starting from the first space, have them move the marker that number of spaces on the ladder or track. The game is over when both children have completed the track.

C. DISTRIBUTION OF MATERIALS

Materials

Appropriate materials for such activities as making:

Collages

Mobiles

Necklaces

Belts

Bracelets

Number booklets

Materials *may* include such items as:

Buttons	Beads
Pipe cleaners	String
Gummed shapes	Yarn
Sheets of colored paper	Rubber bands
Cotton balls	Paper clips
Popsicle sticks	Straws
Tongue depressors	Macaroni
Beans	Bottle caps
Toothpicks	

1. Ask a child to hand out from a large collection specified numbers of each object, to each child at a table. Say, "Give everybody 3 buttons." Check by asking, "Does everybody have 3 buttons?"
2. Tell child to count the number of children, including himself, in a small group by touching each child on the shoulder. Tell child to get enough straws to give one to each child. Check by asking, "Does every child have a straw?"

D. CRAFT ACTIVITIES (See Soc. 7.21)

1. Number Mobiles (*Group Size:* 1, 5)

Materials

Wire coathanger and strings

Buttons

Feathers

Springs

Beads

Paper circles

Paper clips

Help children make a 3-mobile using 3 each of everything, such as 3 buttons, 3 paper clips, 3 feathers. Help child attach 3 objects to each string, by pasting or otherwise. Follow the same procedure for other numbers.

2.   Number Collages

Materials

Same as above

Construction paper

Help children make a 4-collage using 4 each of assorted materials.

5.44 MEANINGS OF ZERO
GROUP SIZE: 2, 5

Behavioral Goal

Children identify and label the empty set as *zero*.

Procedure

A. BEAN BAG THROW

Materials

3 to 4 bean bags

A container or target

A deck of numeral cards with 6 each, marked 0, 1, 2, 3

1. Invite several children to play Bean Bag Throw.
2. Model the game. Say, "We take two turns. I draw one card. What number did I draw? Yes, it's a 3. That means I throw 3 bean bags. Now I draw another card for my second turn. What number did I draw? Yes, it's a zero. Zero means nothing. So I throw no bean bags. Let's begin the game."
3. Supervise the game until it is clear that the children understand the meaning.

B. VARIATIONS OF BEAN BAG THROW

1. Children draw 2 cards at once and figure the total number of throws.
2. Each child keeps a tally of number of turns he takes on individual slates or sheets of paper. See Math. 5.90.

Other Games

1. Add a zero to die and spinner games in Math. 5.42.
2. Add an empty plate and numeral cards for zero to the numeral games in Math. 5.50.
3. See Math 5.81 for addition with symbol zero.
4. See Math. 5.82 for substraction with symbol zero.

Further Reference

Mathematics 5.42, 5.50, 5.81, 5.82, 5.90

5.45 TALLIES AND GRAPHS
GROUP SIZE: 1, 2, 5

Behavioral Goals

Children develop number-recording methods by tally and by graph.

Procedure

A. TALLYING

Materials

Chalk

Chalkboard

1. Demonstrate tallying procedure; for example, in taking attendance, make chalk tallies on chalkboard, always making the fifth tally a horizontal line, through the other 4 lines.
2. Initiate children's use of tallies, in taking attendance or where there is a need to keep track of the maximum number of turns a child may have in a game. For example, if a child may take 5 turns at a spinner in a game before he relinquishes his turn, or if a game ends after 5 rounds, appoint one child to keep the tally on an individual chalkboard or on paper.
3. Tell children, "We need to keep track of the number of turns," or "We need to know when the game ends." Show children how to make tally marks. Show children how to put a horizontal line across 4 tally marks, for the fifth tally.

B. GRAPHS (see Soc. 7.11)

Materials

Pipe cleaners in 4 colors, 25 of each

Gummed squares in same 4 colors

4 pieces of construction paper in same colors

1 graph, squared off to fit the gummed squares

1. Let children select 1 pipe cleaner to make a bracelet for the right hand, after a session with movement or dance.
2. Ask each child to select a gummed square the same color as his bracelet.
3. Ask children to take turns pasting their squares on a graph, all the squares of each color in a separate column, building up from the baseline.

4. Prepare the graph as follows, extending the paper if necessary.

5. Ask children how they could check the graph and give them time to try to figure it out. If children make no suggestions, tell them to check the graph by counting the number of pipe cleaner bracelets of each color.

C. OTHER GRAPH AND TALLY POSSIBILITIES:

(1) Record children's choices of favorite pudding flavors.
(2) Record a child's choice of classroom activities during a week. Assign one color square to each of 4 or 5 selected activities. Have 2 or 3 children complete a graph during the same week and interpret their graphs to each other at the end of the week.
(3) Record the number of seed sprouts visible daily during the second week after planting. See Sci. 6.31.

Further Reference

Science 6.31

Sociology 7.11

Geography 8.20

5.50 NUMERALS
GROUP SIZE: 1, 2, 5

Behavioral Goals

1. Children associate numerals with the number of objects in a set.
2. Children name numerals.

Procedure

Steps under B may not be necessary for some children. To find out, start with the diagnostic check specified in A.

A. DIAGNOSTIC CHECK

Materials

10 plates with sets of objects 1 to 9

Two of a set of 7 objects

10 numeral cards 1 to 9

Two of numeral 7

1. Set out in random order the 10 plates with sets of objects.
2. Give a child the 10 numeral cards. Tell him to place them on the plate that has that number of objects.
3. Check child's completed work to ascertain his numeral learning.
4. Skip B for those children who show mastery in A.

B. NUMERALS AND SETS OF OBJECTS

Materials

About 15 plates

Variety of objects to put on the plate, such as beads, pegs, miniature animals

Numeral cards, about 4 each of numerals 1, 2, 3, 4, 5

Rubber stamp numerals and stamp pad

Flannel numerals

Magnetic numerals

Pencil

Magic marker

Crayons

Paper

Typewriter

1. Give each child a plate. Say to one child, "Pick out 4 things." Say to the other child, "Pick out 3 things."
2. Say to each child, "Let's check. Do you have 4 things? Do you have 3 things?"
3. Ask each child, "Can you find a numeral card in this deck that shows your number?" Help children, if necessary.
4. Follow this procedure for numbers 1 through 5.
5. After children are stable with numerals 1 through 5, continue this procedure for numerals 6 to 9.

C. FIND THE CARD GAME

Materials

Spinner or dice and a set of numeral cards 1 to 6, 6 of each numeral

1. Give 2 children the spinner or a foam cube, marked as a die with 1 through 6 spots. Give them the deck of numeral cards.
2. Tell them to take turns with the spinner or die. Say, "Find the card that matches the number of spots. Keep the card on your pile." The game ends when all the cards are used.

D. DRAW AND MATCH GAME

Materials

2 decks of cards:

Deck of 30 "spot" cards, 6 each with spots 1 through 5

Deck of 30 numeral cards, 6 each of 1 through 5

Tell one child to draw a card from each deck. If the cards match, he puts them on his pile, keeping both cards. If the cards do not match, he puts them on the bottom of the deck and the other child takes his turn.

E. COUNTING GAMES WITH NUMERALS

Introduce numerals into counting games suggested in Math. 5.42.

Materials

Beans

Tongue depressors

Paste

Boxes

Numeral cards 1 to 9

1. Ask child to select a numeral card. Say, "Paste this number of beans on your stick."
2. After pasting, tell children to put the bean sticks in a box for that number, furnishing boxes numbered 1 to 9.

G. NUMBER BOOKLETS (see Soc. 7.21)

Materials

Assorted objects

Cut-outs

Materials of various textures

Construction paper

1. Offer child premarked booklet, with numerals written on pages to signify number of objects to be pasted.
2. Offer child booklet and ask him to specify number of objects to be pasted on each page, such as a *Number 2* book.
3. Ask child to write or stamp numerals on each page to indicate number of objects in the set on page.

5.51 WRITING NUMERALS
GROUP SIZE: 1, 2, 5

Behavioral Goal

Children stamp, type or write numerals.

Procedure

Materials

Numeral chart indicating direction of writing strokes

4 X 6 inch cards, 10 per child

Numeral stamps, 0 through 9

Stamp pad

Gummed seals, such as animals, circles, squares

1. Tape a numeral chart to a wall at child's eye level, to show shape of numeral and direction of writing strokes.
2. Divide each card by a horizontal line across the middle. Stamp a numeral, 1 through 5, on bottom half of card.
3. Invite a child to complete the card by pasting that number of gummed seals on the top half of the card.
4. Invite child to make a set of cards by himself.
5. Start with numeral cards 1 through 5. Later, add cards 6 through 10.

A. STENCILING NUMERALS

Materials

Sandpaper	Crayons
Pencils	Magic Markers
Scissors	Paper

1. Prepare sandpaper stencils of numerals.
2. Invite children to practice writing numerals by tracing stencils.
3. Offer magic markers or crayons for writing numerals.

B. TRACING AND COPYING NUMERALS

Materials

Duplicated sheets of numerals for children to trace and copy

Magic markers

Crayons or pencils

Invite children to practice tracing and copying numerals.

5.52 ORDINAL SEQUENCE
GROUP SIZE: 6, ALL

Behavioral Goal

Children arrange numerals in the ordinal sequence.

Procedure

A. LINE-UP GAME (To be used when lines are formed for dismissal or otherwise)

Materials

1 set green numeral cards 1 to 10

1 set red numeral cards 1 to 10

Additional sets, if needed

1. Distribute 1 set of numeral cards to boys and another set to girls.
2. Tell children who get the number 1 cards that they are leaders of their lines.
3. Tell each leader to call his line, announcing his color first, calling each number in turn.
4. After lines are formed, say, "Your number helps you remember your place in line. You're first, you're second, you're third . . ."

B. WHAT'S MY NUMBER GAME

Materials

8½ × 11 inch construction paper, 5 pieces

Magic marker

Yarn cut into 18 inch lengths

Stapler

1. Write one large numeral on each paper, using numerals 1 through 5.
2. Fasten yarn to paper, necklace-style.
3. Invite 5 children to get a number tag. Place the yarn around the child's neck, with the number on his back.
4. Invite another child to read the numeral tags and place the group in order from first to fifth.
5. Check. Say, "You are first in line. What number do you think you have? Now look at it and see if you are right."
6. Check children in order, at first. Later, check positions randomly.

5.53 ONE-MORE GAME

Behavioral Goal

Children order numbers by the relation of "one more."

Procedure

Number Path Game

Materials

12 X 14 foot length brown wrapping paper

Magic marker

Masking tape

1. Draw 12 "stepping stones" on brown wrapping paper by making circles with a 6 inch diameter, 6 inches apart.
2. Number these "stepping stones" in order from zero to ten, leaving last circle blank.
3. Tape this paper number path securely to floor, so that numbers read from left to right.
4. Invite several children to play the Number Path Game.
5. Ask one child to take a few steps on the number path.
6. Ask group, "What number is he standing on?" Check by asking child to read the number on which he is standing.
7. Ask group, "if he takes one more step on what number will he be standing?"
8. Ask child to check. "Take one more step."

Variations

1. Invite 3 children to line up on steps 1, 2, and 3.
    a. Ask children, "On what numbers are you standing? One, two, three, that's right."
    b. Say, "Everybody take one more step. Now, let's check your numbers. Two, three, four. That's right."
    c. Repeat Item b, several times, maintaining a brisk pace.
2. Invite several children to watch while one child finds a place on the number path.
    a. Have group close their eyes. Tell child to move 2 steps forward.
    b. Ask group to guess what number child is standing on, before looking.
    c. Check by having child read the number.

Mathematics 5.53

Further Reference
Mathematics 5.42, 5.50

5.60 ORDERING OBJECTS BY LENGTH: MR. LONG GAME
GROUP SIZE: 2, 5

Behavioral Goals

1. Children order a group of objects by length.
2. Children verbalize terms of length.

Procedure

Materials

Shoe box

Materials of varied length, such as:

Pipe cleaners	Wooden dowels
Straws	Sticks

1. Cut a window, large enough for a hand to reach in, at one end of shoe box.
2. Invite 2 children to play game.
3. Place sticks in a box and say, "This game is called Mr. Long. Each player takes one stick from the box. Place your sticks against the box like this. If you have Mr. Long, you win both sticks." Model procedure for comparing lengths.
4. If sticks of the same length are drawn, let children make a rule, such as, "Each keep their own," or "Return both sticks and draw again."
5. Game ends when all sticks are used.

Variations

1. Increase number of players. If there are two Mr. Long's, let children make a rule.
2. Reverse game to Mr. Short, in which shortest stick wins.
3. Ordering by length in craft activities (see Soc. 7.21).

Key Language

Long	Short
Longer	Shorter
Longest	Shortest

Mathematics 5.60

Further Reference
Science 6.10
Sociology 7.21

5.70 ARBITRARY LINEAR MEASUREMENT
GROUP SIZE: 2, 5

Behavioral Goal

Children use arbitrary measures, such as new crayons, straws, or spoons.

Procedure

Materials

Art work

Measuring materials, such as:

New crayons	Tongue depressors
Plastic spoons	Straws
Counting cubes	Paper clips
Pipe cleaners	Rubber bands
Strips of oaktag	

Box for measuring materials

Framing materials, such as:

Roll of gummed tape	Paste
Ribbon	Stapler
Cash register tape	Scissors

1. Invite several children to select painting or other art work to frame.
2. Demonstrate measuring procedure:
   a. Select one kind of item from measuring box, such as crayons.
   b. Lay these end-to-end across the top of one painting, saying, "We start at the edge." for the last segment measured, say, "We only need a half (or some, or a little bit) of this last crayon, but we'll use a whole one anyway."
   c. Count aloud the number of items used. Say, "I have 6 crayons."
   d. Take the 6 crayons to the cutting table. Lay out the crayons end-to-end on the tape, ribbon, or strips, counting them. Say, "I still have 6 crayons."
   e. Cut the framing material.

      f.   Demonstrate the pasting or stapling procedure.

      g.   Trim the framing material, if necessary, saying, "It's too long because we didn't need all of that last crayon."

3.   Ask each child to select one of the measuring materials to use for his measurement.

4.   Let children discover that the same measurement usually applies to the opposite sides of their art work, but may not apply to the other two sides.

5.   Let children discover which items in the measuring box are more efficient than others.

6.   Vary the measuring materials occasionally offering more efficient items such as oaktag or construction paper strips exactly 4 inches long, and less efficient items such as rubber bands or pipe cleaners.

7.   Invite a child who was skillful with arbitrary linear measurement to use standard linear measurement (see Math. 5.71).

Further Reference

Mathematics 5.71

5.71 STANDARD LINEAR MEASUREMENT
GROUP SIZE: 1, 2, 5

Behavioral Goals

1. Children acquire selected measurement vocabulary.
2. Children experience teacher modeling of measurement.
3. Children use standard measuring devices in playful situations, such as block building.

Procedure

Materials

Standard measuring devices, such as:

Strips of oaktag in 6 and 12 inch lengths, marked in inches

Rulers in 6 and 12 inch lengths

A yardstick

Measuring tapes

1. Use linear measurement for such classroom purposes as decorating a bulletin board, a mailbox for Valentine's Day or other holiday, or measuring children for making belts, bracelets, or Indian headbands.
2. Model uses of the ruler in context whenever convenient, without expecting children to copy standard measurement behavior. Use key language.
3. Provide measurement devices for such children's activities as carpentry, block play, and housekeeping play, for manipulation and individual exploration.
4. Measuring Lines

Variations

Materials

Construction paper with lines of different lengths drawn in exact inches but without numerals

Rulers

Stamp pad and number stamps

1. Draw lines on construction paper, exactly 2 through 8 inches long.
2. Invite a child to measure the length of each line with a ruler and to stamp the numeral on that line.

Key Language

Longer than	Edge
Shorter than	Measure
Higher or taller than	Count
Ruler	Inch
Yardstick	

5.72 SOME STANDARD MEASURES FOR LIQUIDS
GROUP SIZE: 1, 2, 5

Behavioral Goal

Children use and label some standard measures for liquids.

Procedure

Materials

Large dishpan or bowl

Food coloring for water

Funnels

Measuring containers: ½ cup, 1 cup, quart

5 identical 8-oz. glasses or transparent plastic tumblers

Containers such as:

8-oz. plastic nursing bottle

1 cup and 1 quart milk containers with tops cut off

Pouring pitchers

1. Invite several children to play with water and some standard liquid measures.
2. After considerable unstructured water play, begin to pose such problems as:
   a. "Pour this quart of blue water into these 6 cups. Can you fill all 6 cups?"
   b. "Pour the red water from these 4 cups into the quart container. Is the quart container full? Would it hold another cup of water?"
3. Pebble Tally
   a. Invite 2 children to fill quart containers, one with a 1 cup measure, the other with a ½ cup measure.
   b. Give them a box of pebbles and tell each child to take out a pebble every time he pours a full measure into his quart container.
   c. Help children check, then count pebbles by reversing the pouring from the quart container to the measuring cup, returning a pebble to the box each time.
   d. See Math. 5.45, working with tallies and graphs, for children who are interested.

e. Encourage children to repeat procedures until they begin to notice that the ½ cup measure requires twice as many pebbles as the 1 cup measure. If children do not notice the difference in number of pebbles, try to elicit this information from them by asking, "Do you both have the same number of pebbles?"

Further Reference

Mathematics 5.45

5.80 COMBINING SETS UP TO A TOTAL OF 10
GROUP SIZE: 2, 5

Behavioral Goals

1. Children associate a number with sets of a given size.
2. Children join 2 sets and apply a number to the newly created set.

Procedure

Materials

Two colors of paper cups and a box of straws

Paper plate or tray

1. Invite 2 children who show mastery of counting in Math. 5.42 to play the game.
2. Tell one child to pick a few pink cups. Tell the other child to pick a few blue cups.
3. Ask each child how many cups he has.
4. Ask both children to put their cups on the tray.
5. Ask, "How many straws will we need for all these cups?"
6. Accept the response without checking.
7. Tell the children to count out the number of straws they need.
8. Ask, "How do we tell whether we have the right number of straws?" Suggest putting a straw in each cup if the children don't make this suggestion.
9. Help the children check and correct their estimate, if necessary.

5.81 ADDITION USING SYMBOLS
GROUP SIZE: 2, 5

Behavioral Goals

1. Children associate a numeral with the number of objects in a set.
2. Children join sets and apply a number to the newly created set.
3. Children use symbols, *plus* (+) and *equals* (=), in making an addition equation.
4. Children partition a set into 2 groups and identify the number in each subset.

Procedure

Materials

1 deck of numeral cards 1 through 4

1 deck of numeral cards 1 through 5

1 deck of numeral cards 1 through 9

Symbol cards + and =

2 plates

1 tray

1 box of 15 attractive objects

1. Invite 2 children who have shown mastery of counting and of numerals through 9 to work.
2. Ask one child to pick a numeral card from the 1 through 4 deck. Ask the other child to pick a card from the 1 through 5 deck.
3. Tell each child to put his card on a paper plate and to put that number of objects on his plate.
4. Ask each child to check by counting aloud.
5. Say, "We are going to do some addition. We are going to join this set of 3 things with this set of 5 things. This plus sign tells us to put things together."
6. Start an equation with the cards: 3 + 5.
7. Point to the cards. Say, "This means we take 3 things and put them together with 5 things."
8. Ask children to combine their sets. Say, "You put your 3 things together with your 5 things on the tray."

9. Ask one child to "Count these things and tell us how many things there are altogether."
10. Ask the other child to check the count, and find the numeral card for this number.
11. Place this card to the right of the other cards, leaving a space for the equals sign.

3 + 5   8

12. Summarize the procedure so far by saying, "This means that when you put 3 things together with 5 things, you have 8 things. We need one more card. This is an equals sign." Point to the blank space between the 3 + 5 and the 8. Say, "This is where we put the equals sign."
13. Put the equals sign in place in the equation: 3 + 5 = 8. Point to each card in turn and say, "Three things together with 5 things gives us 8 things."
14. Repeat steps 1 through 13 several times, for practice, using different numbers.
15. Give teacher role to a child who shows mastery of the addition operation.

Independent Activity

A. GET RICH GAME

Materials

Spinner

Die

Play money dollar bills

1. Invite a small group of children to play the game and appoint one child as banker.
2. Demonstrate the rules of the game.
   a. Each player spins the spinner (numerals through 6), and the die (numerals through 6).
   b. He tells the banker, "I have a 3 and a 4. Pay me 7 dollars."
   c. Banker counts out 2 piles of dollars, 3 and 4, and checks by counting. If the count is correct, banker pays money.
3. Variation: Add zero to die and spinner. Key language: zero means nothing. See Math. 5.44 for uses of zero.

139

B. GROUPING OBJECTS

Materials

Counting cubes or wooden beads

Papers with line drawn down center

Numeral cards 4 through 10

1. Invite child to work with beads or cubes and a set of paper plates.
2. Ask child to pick a numeral card, the same number of paper plates, and place that number of cubes on each plate.
3. Tell the child to find out how many different ways he can arrange the cubes on the plates, varying the size of the groups placed on each side of the line. Tell him to take more plates if he needs them. For numeral 4, a complete set of groupings on the paper plates would look like this:

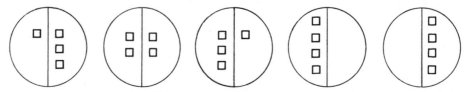

4. Accept what the child does even though he may not make all possible combinations. For further instruction, use the following craft activity.

C. MAKING A GROUPING BOOK

Materials

Sheets of paper folded in half

Numeral cards 4 through 10

Numeral stamps and stamp pad

Gummed circles

Wet sponge

1. Invite a child to copy the groupings he made on plates by pasting gummed circles on each half of the folded paper, and stamping numerals to show his groupings.
2. If he has omitted some groupings, suggest these to him by stamping a numeral on one side and letting him complete the sheet.

5.82 SUBTRACTION USING SYMBOLS
GROUP SIZE: 2, 5

Behavioral Goals

1. Children associate a numeral with the number of objects in a set.
2. Children partition sets into 2 groups, remove 1 group and apply a number to the remaining group.
3. Children use symbols, minus (–) and equals (=) in making a subtraction equation.

Procedure

Materials

　1 deck of numerals 1 through 4

　1 deck of numerals 5 through 9

　1 deck of numerals 1 through 9

　1 tray

　1 paper plate

　Symbol cards for minus (–) and equals (=)

　1 box of attractive objects (about 15)

1. Ask one child to pick a card from the 5 through 9 deck and to make a set of that number of objects on the tray.
2. Ask the other child to pick a card from the 1 through 4 deck and place it on the plate.
3. Say, "Last time we did addition. This is different. We are going to do subtraction. Some people call it 'take away.' We start with 8 things here (point to tray), take 2 away (point to the number on the plate), and then find out how many are left."
4. Show the minus sign (–). Say, "This minus sign tells us to take things away."
5. Start the equation 8 – 2, saying, "This means we start with 8 things, and we take away 2 things."
6. Ask one child to take 2 things off the tray and put them on the plate.
7. Ask one child, "How many things are left on the tray?" Ask the other child to check and find the numeral card for this number.
8. Place this card to the right of the other cards, leaving a space for the equals sign.

$$8 \quad - \quad 2 \qquad 6$$

9. Summarize the procedure so far by saying, "This means that when there are 8 things and you take away 2 things, there are 6 things left."
10. Say, "We need one more card." Hold up the equals sign. Ask, "Do you remember what we called this?"
11. Say, "Yes, this is the equals sign. Where does it belong?" Allow one child to put it in place.

$$8 - 2 = 6$$

12. Point to each card in turn and say, "Eight things take away 2 things leaves us 6 things."
13. Repeat steps 1 through 12 for practice, using different numbers.
14. Give teacher role to child who shows mastery of subtraction operation.

Independent Activity

Lucky Beans Game

Procedure

Materials

A box of beans (or beads or other small objects)

2 foam rubber cubes, one marked with plus and minus signs, the other with numerals 0 through 5 (or 2 spinners)

1. Ask each child to take 10 beans out of the box and place them on a plate in front of him.
2. Model the rules of the game. Throw the number die first. Say, "My number is three." Throw the other die for sign. Say, "I got a minus sign. I have to take away 3." Put 3 beans into the box. Tell children the game ends when one child has no more beans.
3. Supervise the game until it is clear that the children can verbalize the results of their throws.

Key Language

Plus	Minus
Add	Subtract
Take away	Zero
Nothing	Sign

5.90 CONSERVATION OF NUMBER

Behavioral Goal

Children conserve number despite nonnumerical changes.

Procedure

Materials

8 to 10 red checkers

Same number of white poker chips

1. Arrange the 2 sets in matching rows:

   Checkers   0 0 0 0 0 0

   Chips   0 0 0 0 0 0

2. Ask child, "Are there more checkers or more chips or are there the same number of each?"
3. Help child to establish the size of the 2 sets as equal—either by touching or counting.
4. Bunch the row of chips but leave the row of checkers untouched:

   Checkers   0 0 0 0 0 0

   Chips   000000

5. Repeat question, as in 2, above.
6. Help child check his response by one-to-one matching.
7. See Chart D for sequence of variations.
   a. Bunch one row.
   b. Spread one row.
   c. Group one row.
   d. Spread one group.
   e. Stack one group.
   f. Substitution of 1 or 2 objects. For example: same object in a different color, different-sized object.
   g. Bunch set of small objects and compare to set of large objects.
8. Invite a nonconserving child to work with you, after watching you work with a conserving child.
9. Invite a nonconserving child to work with a conserving child, as you watch, and add verbalization, if you think it is needed.

CHART D: CONSERVATION OF NUMBER

Sequence of Variations	Starting Position	Final Position
Variation A (bunch)	0 0 0 0 0 0 0 0 0 0 0 0	0 0 0 0 0 0 0 0 0 0 0 0
Variation B (spread)	0 0 0 0 0 0 0 0 0 0 0 0	0 0 0 0 0 0 0 0 0 0 0 0 0
Variation C (group)	0 0 0 0 0 0 0 0 0 0 0 0	0 0 0 0 0 0 0 00 0 0 0

Variation D (regroup)	0 0
	 0 0 0 0
	
	 0 0 0 0
	 0 0
		0
		 0 0 0 0
		 0 0 0
		 0
		         0 0
		         0

Variation E (stack)	0 0 0 0 0 0 0 0 0 0 0 0	0 0 0 0 0 0 0
Variation F (substitution)	0 0 0 0 0 0 0 0 0 0 0 0	0 0 0 0 0 0 0 0 0 0 0 0
Variation G (substitute and spread)	0 0 0 0 0 0 0 0 0 0 0 0	0 0 0 0 0 0 0 0 0 0 0 0 0

Science

6.00   Goals in Science
6.01   Chart Summary of Science Materials
6.10   Identify Properties of Objects
6.11   Experiment to Identify Properties of Objects
6.20   Transforming Food Materials
6.21   Transforming Materials
6.22   Planting Seeds
6.23   Caring for Animals
6.30   Prediction
6.40   Sort and Classify

6.00 GOALS IN SCIENCE

Science learnings of young children begin with developing the skills of *observation* and verbal *communication.* In the initial stages, the teaching procedures emphasize manipulation and action in order to feature perceptual clarity and vocabulary expansion. The program specifies activities which lead toward the goals of *sorting, classification, experimentation,* and *prediction.*

Behavioral Goals

1. Children use their five senses (auditory, gustatory, olfactory, tactile, and visual) to identify the observable properties of objects.
2. Children label properties.
3. Children sort and classify objects based upon physical properties.
4. Children use different classification patterns with the same group of objects.
5. Children experiment with interaction processes to discover properties of objects.
6. Children classify objects in terms of interaction with other objects.
7. Children predict the changes or the sequence of events as a result of interaction.
8. Children tally and graph observed data.

CHART A: SUMMARY OF SCIENCE MATERIALS

Physical Property	Activity	Materials		Key Language	
1. Rigidity	*Soc. 7.20-7.22* Crafts: collages, books, mobiles, woodworking	wood cotton balls	metal plush fabrics	hard fluid frozen pour	soft freeze melted
	Sci. 6.21 Water play	sponge water rock assortment	foam rubber refrigerator	squeeze stiff pliant yielding	solid fold unyielding yields
	Soc. 7.20-7.22 Crafts: collages, books, mobiles, woodworking	pipe cleaners rigid plastic spoons and forks tongue depressors steel rod	paper washers copper wire	flexible bend straight break	firm inflexible twist crooked fold
2. Surface texture	*Soc. 7.20-7.22* Crafts: collages, books, mobiles, woodworking	wood sandpaper styrofoam corrugated paper aluminum foil	marble rope wire yarn	hairy rough bumpy slippery scratchy	smooth flat shaggy nap porous
3. Heat	*Sci. 6.20* Cooking *Sci. 6.21* Freezing and melting water	water glass tumblers food materials	ice cubes hot plate refrigerator	icy frozen heat steam	freeze melt cool boiling
4. Size, shape, and color	*Math. 5.11* Sorting objects *Soc. 7.20, 7.21* Sorting and classifying in crafts *Sci. 6.11, 6.21* Properties of objects *Soc. 7.20-7.22* Crafts: collages, books, mobiles, woodworking	assorted balls: ping pong tennis hard rubber soft rubber paper fabric assorted lengths of materials: pipe cleaners rope yarn wooden dowels	golf cotton styrofoam plastic cardboard rubber straws string sticks	round fat big roll color names long longer shorter heavy stretch bend	flat thin little bounce short longest shortest light knot tie

Physical Property	Activity	Materials	Key Language	
	Math. 5.11 Sorting objects	property blocks	round triangular big color names	square fat little thin
	Sci. 6.10, 6.11 Properties of objects	water freezer containers	frozen cube large	solid small
	Sci. 6.21 Freezing and melting water			
5. Consistency	*Lang. 4.10* Playdough *Sci. 6.20* Cooking *Soc. 7.21* Finger painting *Soc. 7.30* Art	salt flour water coloring cooking ingredients soap flakes coloring liquid starch poster paints poster paints chalk clay	sticky crumbly thin thick pasty jellied solidified clear vivid	smooth lumpy watery thicker creamy fluid bright muddy hazy
6. Buoyancy	*Sci. 6.21* Water play	water variety of objects that sink or float	float quickly suspend	sink slowly surface
7. Odor	*Sci. 6.20* Cooking *Lang. 4.10* Play with classroom materials	fruits, such as: oranges lemons cantaloupe watermelon vinegar cheeses herbs spices play materials	smell pleasant odor fruity sharp aroma It smells like	fragrance unpleasant fumes scorched spicy
8. Taste	*Sci. 6.20* Cooking *Sci. 6.21* Transforming materials	cooking ingredients stove refrigerator	sweet sour salty It tastes like	sweeter bitter sugary
9. Auditory properties	*Music 3.41* Auditory discrimination of musical instruments *Sci. 6.11* Properties of objects	musical instruments bells buzzer balls rattles boxes plastic jars varied sizes of tin cans, rubber, metal, and woodtipped strikers	hollow rattle buzz soft striker	solid ring loud sound chime
10. Absorbency	*Sci. 6.11* Experimenting with materials	blotters sponges foam rubber fabric metal wood food color wax paper paper towels	absorbs dry damp	squeezing wet waxy

6.10 IDENTIFY PROPERTIES OF OBJECTS
GROUP SIZE: 1, 2, 5

Behavioral Goals

1. Children use their five senses (auditory, gustatory, olfactory, tactile, and visual) to identify the observable properties of concrete objects.
2. Children label the properties identified.
3. Children learn new name labels.
4. Children write numerals, words, and sentences.

Procedure

Materials

Tray	Tape
Paper	Stapler
Paste	Scissors
Boxes	Crayons
Letter stamps	Stamp pad
Numeral stamps	Pencils

Hard materials:

Buttons	Sticks
Wood	Bolts
Plastic discs	Washers
Paper clips	Nuts

Soft materials:

Cotton cloth	Rayon
Cotton batting	Yarn
Sponges	String
Velvet	Silk
Woolcloth	Plush

1. Invite children to make a "Hard-Soft Book," or to make two collages, one of hard materials, the other of soft materials.
2. Help children to sort and label materials, to classify objects as hard or

soft and to learn any name labels which may be new to them. See Lang. 4.13.

3. Check children's classification and if necessary, help them to reclassify, before pasting, taping, or stapling. Ignore errors in pasting. See Soc. 7.21.

4. After pasting help children who are interested, to write or stamp letters or numbers on the pages, to number the pages, to head pages "hard things," "soft things," or in other ways. See Lang. 4.20 and 4.22.

5. See Sci. 6.01 for other properties and materials that can be used for projects of this type.

6. Additional projects requiring identification and labeling of objects include mobiles, bulletin board exhibits, classroom collection boxes and mystery bags. See Lang. 6.40 and Math. 5.11, Eureka Game.

7. Let children solve problems such as how to make some objects adhere to the paper, how to fasten a book and how to find additional items for a class of subjects.

Further Reference

Language 4.13, 4.20, 4.22, 4.60

Mathematics 5.11

Science 6.01

Sociology 7.21

6.11 EXPERIMENT TO IDENTIFY PROPERTIES OF OBJECTS
GROUP SIZE: 1, 2, 5

Behavioral Goals

1. Children experiment to identify properties of concrete objects.
2. Children label the properties identified
3. Children write numerals, words and sentences.

Procedure

Materials

Boxes

Inclined plane, made of wood strip and upright

Collection of materials such as:

Wheels	Paper clips
Balls	Hardware nuts
Blocks	Plastic plate
Pencils	Ruler

For additional collections, see Sci. 6.01

1. Invite children to make collection boxes, mobiles, exhibits, collages, or books.
2. Offer children a tray of selected materials to classify objects for such properties as:
    a. Light—heavy;
    b. Sink—float;
    c. Absorption of liquids versus nonabsorption of liquids;
    d. Rigidity—nonrigidity;
    e. Elasticity—nonelasticity;
    f. Magnetic—nonmagnetic;
    g. Compressible—noncompressible;
    h. Things that roll—things that do not roll.
3. An example of a teaching sequence follows, for "things that roll":
    a. Invite children to make an inclined plane at the carpentry bench, to experiment to find out which objects roll and which do not. See Soc. 7.22 for the carpentry project.
    b. Offer children boxes and a tray of objects, some of which are round and some of which are not.

    c.   Suggest that children experiment with the inclined plane, in order to classify things that roll and things that do not roll.

    d.   Ask children to sort objects into 2 boxes labeled "Things that Roll" and "Things that Do Not Roll." Let children write or letter-stamp these labels, if they wish to.

    e.   Suggest children find additional objects in the classroom to sort into these 2 boxes.

    f.   Help children use the contents of each box to make an exhibit, a book, a collage, a mobile, or other end-product.

4.   See Sci. 6.01 for additional materials and properties.

5.   Additional projects can include things that bounce versus things that do not bounce, things that rattle or ring versus things that do not, things with a low pitch versus things with a high pitch.

Further Reference

Language 4.20, 4.22

Science 6.01

Sociology 7.22

6.20 TRANSFORMING FOOD MATERIALS
GROUP SIZE: 2, 5

Behavioral Goals

1. Children identify and label changes in food materials as evidence of interaction.
2. Children use hindsight to compare food materials after interaction.
3. Children match a set of objects to a duplicate set.
4. Children narrate classroom experiences in sequence.
5. Children read and write sentences and stories.

Procedure

Materials

2 sets of any of the following:

Fresh oranges and an orange squeezer, to make orange juice

Apples, water, sugar, and a hot plate, to make apple sauce

Pancake mix, butter, eggs, milk, and a waffle iron or hot plate and skillet, to make waffles or pancakes

Cranberries, sugar, blender to make cranberry sauce, or a hot plate and a saucepan

Fresh heavy cream and a closed jar (or a bowl and eggbeater), to make butter

Instant pudding, or jello, milk, a bowl and eggbeater, to make pudding

Koolaid, water, sugar, and mixing spoon or closed jar to make sweet drinks

Frozen fruit juice, water, spoon, can opener, and closed jar, to make juice drink

Confectioner's sugar, water, bowl, and spoon (vanilla, food coloring and melted butter are optional) to make icing for cookies or cake

1. Assemble two sets of ingredients, each on a separate tray.
2. Help children label materials.
3. Help children identify properties of the objects by such activities as taste, touch, sight, smell, lifting, shaking, tapping, and rolling.
4. Help children match objects on the reference tray to the duplicate set, to establish the equivalence of the two sets. See Math. 5.12.

5. An example of a teaching sequence:
   a. Invite children to make orange juice from fresh juice oranges.
   b. Help children cut and squeeze the oranges.
   c. In the process elicit observations and interject vocabulary without slowing the activity.
   d. Compare the used ingredients and the end product with the duplicate set of unused materials to help children identify and label differences.
   e. Invite children to compose a story about the activity for a duplicated booklet. See Lang. 4.64.
   f. Invite children to tape record a narration of the experience. See Lang. 4.11.

Further Reference

Language 4.11, 4.13, 4.64

Mathematics 5.12

6.21 TRANSFORMING MATERIALS

Behavioral Goals

1. Children identify and label changes in materials as evidence of interaction.
2. Children use hindsight to compare materials after interaction.
3. Children match a set of objects to a duplicate set.
4. Children narrate classroom experiences in sequence.
5. Children read and write sentences and stories.

Procedure

1. Assemble materials on an uncluttered table.
2. Have 2 sets of materials, 1 set to remain unused on a tray, for comparison with the other set of transformed materials. See Sci. 6.20.
3. Invite a few children to play with the materials.
4. Suggest basic procedure to children wherever it is not self-evident or where children are unfamiliar with the process.
5. Accept children's suggestions and variations wherever possible.
6. Use some of the following activities as content for classroom booklets. See Lang. 4.64.

Transformation activities

A. SOAP BUBBLES

Materials

Detergent or soapflakes	Food coloring
Bowls	Water
Eggbeater	Straws

1. Let children use eggbeaters to whip the soap bubbles and straws to blow them.
2. Remind children to compare the unused set of materials with the used set and verbalize the differences.

B. PLAYDOUGH

Materials

Salt	Flour
Water	Paper

Food coloring	Bowls

Spoons

1. See Lang. 4.10 for procedure.
2. Combine 2 parts flour to 1 part salt with enough water to make a smooth dough which can be handled without sticking.
3. Remind children to compare the unused set of materials with the used set, and verbalize the differences.

C. FINGER PAINT

Materials

Liquid starch	Water
Soap flakes	Bowl
Tempera paint	Spoon

Egg beater

1. Combine materials to make a thick paste, experimenting to get the desired consistency. Beat with egg beater to whip materials into smooth blend.
2. Remind children to compare the used set of materials with the unused set, and verbalize the differences.
3. Encourage finger painting with the freshly made paint.

D. FLOUR PASTE

Materials

Flour	Bowl
Water	Spoon or fork

Preservative

1. Combine ingredients to make a smooth paste.
2. To prevent mold, add a drop of oil of wintergreen or other preservative.
3. Use the paste for craft activities.
4. Remind children to compare used materials with unused set.
5. Help them identify and label changes in materials.
6. See Soc. 7.20 and 7.21 for selection of craft activities requiring paste.

E. PAPIER-MÂCHÉ

Materials

Flour	Cardboard core

Newspaper   Water

Spoons   Bowl

1. Help children combine flour and water to make a liquid of the consistency of thin cream.
2. Help children tear newspaper into strips and soak strips in liquid.
3. Have children select a core, such as a cardboard paper towel tube, ball of clay or plastiscene, an empty juice can or loosely balled dry newspaper.
4. Help children cover cores by applying layers of soaked newspaper strips.
5. Arrange drying space.
6. Let interested children add additional layers on the following day.
7. Invite interested children to paint the dry papier-maché.
8. See Soc. 7.20 and 7.21 for suggested craft products.

Further Reference

Language 4.10, 4.64

Mathematics 5.12

Science 6.20

Sociology 7.20, 7.21

6.22 PLANTING SEEDS
GROUP SIZE: 1, 2, 5

Behavioral Goals

1. Children experiment with an interaction process to identify and label properties of matter.
2. Children tally and graph observed data.
3. Children narrate a class experience in sequence, and make booklets.
4. Children make a purchase.
5. Children identify a route from school to store.

Procedure

Materials

Soil	Cotton batting
Water	Garden tools
Tray	Toothpicks
Seeds	Individual planters such as milk cartons

1. Purchase soil and seeds that germinate rapidly, such as radish or lentil, following procedures in Geog. 8.31 and Econ. 9.10.
2. Help children plant their seeds, encouraging them to do as much as they can by themselves.
3. In process, elicit observations and interject vocabulary without slowing the activity. See Lang. 4.10 and 4.13.
4. Help children write or stamp name on wooden markers and place them in planters. See Lang. 4.20.
5. Place planters on a shelf that is protected from extreme changes in temperature.

Variations

1. Plant lima bean seeds in cotton batting in the following way:
   a. Place the seeds 2 inches apart on a layer of cotton.
   b. Cover the seeds with another layer of cotton.
   c. Moisten the wet cotton, but do not saturate it.
   d. Check progress daily, adding water as needed.
2. Plant beans in cotton, as in Variation 1. In addition, plant about a dozen beans in soil, following procedures in steps 2 through 5.
   a. Use a toothpick to mark where each bean is planted in soil.

    b. Prepare 2 charts to show daily record of sprouting, as in Item 5 below, one chart for the cotton bed and one for the soil bed.

    c. Check daily and record sprouting progress. Let children check beans for sprouting by uncovering one bean from the cotton bed and one from the soil bed daily.

3. Follow same procedure as in Variation 1. In addition, plant a group of seeds in another cotton bed, but omit the water. Let the children compare the 2 groups of seeds daily.

4. Use a clear glass tumbler, white blotter paper, and radish seeds.

    a. Place blotter around inside surface of glass, to fit as snugly as possible.

    b. Slip several radish seeds between blotter and glass so that they are held in position against the glass but not at the base.

    c. Place ½ inch of water in glass tumbler. Let children note the absorption of water by the blotter. Help them check seeds daily.

5. Follow Math. 5.45, for tallies or graph. To make a graph of new sprouts daily:

    a. Start a new graph for each planting.

    b. Attach names or photographs of the children responsible for the graph and the planting.

    c. Let children paste gummed green squares in a vertical column to represent the sprouts that are counted each day. Each green square can represent one sprout. If there are too many sprouts, use a gummed yellow circle to represent 5 sprouts.

    d. Give children as much responsibility as they can handle in caring for plants and in keeping the graph current.

6. Variations in graphing and tallying:

    a. Children who can handle numerals may stamp or write numerals on the graph, instead of pasting gummed paper.

    b. Tally marks may be substituted for the gummed paper.

    c. Beans may be pasted, instead of using gummed paper.

7. Making duplicated booklets
Use the contents of this experience for a duplicated booklet, as suggested in Lang. 4.64.

Further Reference

Language 4.10, 4.13, 4.20, 4.64

Mathematics 5.45

Geography 8.31

Economics 9.10

6.23 CARING FOR ANIMALS
GROUP SIZE: 1, 5

Behavioral Goals

1. Children identify attributes of animals by caring for them in the classroom.
2. Children label animal needs and attributes by caring for them.
3. Children classify the survival needs of animals they care for.

Procedure

Materials

Various small, *hardy* animals which can be cared for in cages in the classroom, such as:

Gerbils	White mice
Rabbits	Turtles
Hamsters	Chameleons

Less hardy animals may be cared for with special equipment and the required environment such as temperature control or noise control (this includes tropical fish, tadpoles and chicks)

Cages, or other housing	Cleaning equipment
Animal food	Feeding equipment

1. See Geog. 8.31 for neighborhood walks, if a pet store is within walking distance and if walks are planned, either to acquire an animal or food or other equipment. See also Econ. 9.12, if it is planned for children to participate in making purchases at a pet shop or other store.
2. Involve children in planning to acquire a classroom pet by stories, discussion and photographs.
3. Involve children in preparing the living conditions for a classroom pet before its acquisition.
4. After the classroom pet is acquired, demonstrate care of the pet, verbalizing your action.
5. Feature the animal's needs for protection against overstimulation, too much noise, or handling.
6. Rotate the responsibilities for caring for the classroom pet among the helper chores on the helper chart. See Soc. 7.11.
7. Encourage children's discussion about the properties of the classroom

pet, such as mode of locomotion, eating and elimination habits, visual and tactile properties and reactions to children's holding.

8. Encourage children to raise questions about the classroom pet which require observation and experimentation (only those which are safe for the pet). For example, encourage children to find out what kinds of food the pet will eat, whether it can hear or see, what noises it can make and what kinds of responses it can make.

9. Invite children to tape record their experiences with the classroom pet.

10. Prepare a series of booklets based on children's tape recorded experiences of purchasing and caring for the pet. See Lang. 4.64.

11. If there is more than one kind of classroom pet, such as gerbils and tropical fish, encourage children to identify similarities and differences between them.

12. Encourage children to make simple classifications of animals, based on experience with their own pets and the classroom pets. For example, classification may simply be based on whether the pet is fur-bearing or not, its food habits, patterns of locomotion, or sleeping habits.

Further Reference

Geography 8.31

Economics 9.12

Language 4.64

Sociology 7.11

6.30 PREDICTION
GROUP SIZE: 1, 2, 5

Behavioral Goals

1. Children transform familiar objects and predict changes.
2. Children compare results of transformation with prediction.

Procedure

Materials

Water tumblers	Water
Cooking oil	Salt
Food coloring	Sugar
Paper towel	Yarn
Detergent	String
Talcum powder	Straws

1. Invite children to experiment with materials.
2. Require children to predict what will happen before they experiment. Accept any prediction.
3. Require children to tell you whether their predictions were borne out.
4. An example of a teaching sequence follows:
   a. Give child water, tumblers and collection of such materials as salt, sugar, detergent, yarn, string, paper towel, cooking oil, food coloring.
   b. Tell child to select one material from the collection to put in the water. Ask child to predict what will happen to the material and to the water.
   c. Check his prediction with him.

6.40 SORT AND CLASSIFY
GROUP SIZE: 1, 2, 5

Behavioral Goals

1. Children sort objects according to a specified base.
2. Children classify groups of objects based upon the criteria for sorting.

Procedure

Materials

One set of ten objects (see Sci. 6.01 for suggested materials and properties)

A. FOLLOW-THE-LEADER GAME

1. Collect a set of ten objects that offer a clear contrast of one property, such as big—little.
2. Select one child to be leader. Leader picks one object, states one property, and each player selects an object with the specified property. Give children turns to be leader.
3. Variation: After children develop skill with this game, require selection of 2 simultaneous criteria for sorting. For example, child may select objects that are round and soft, or square and red. See Lang. 4.16 for an appropriate word game.

B. GRAB-BAG GAME

1. Place objects in bag.
2. Select one child to be leader.
3. Have leader reach into bag, grab an object and state how it feels before removing it.
4. Have each child find an object in the bag that feels the same as the one the leader chose.
5. Give children turns to be leaders.

C. HANDS-BEHIND-YOUR-BACK GAME

1. Tell child to place hands behind his back.
2. Place one hard object in each child's right hand and a soft object in his left hand.
3. Request all soft objects to be placed on table, by saying, "You have one *hard* object and one *soft* object. Put the *soft* object on this table."
4. Request that hard objects be placed in another pile.
5. Ask a child to check each group for accuracy.

D. COLLAGE, BOOKLETS, MOBILES

Invite children to make a *single purpose* collage, such as a "soft" collage using only soft materials. See Soc. 7.21.

E. CLASSIFICATION

1. Use a collection of objects for classification practice when there is a function to be served. For example, classify a collection of objects as *writing tools*, to prepare for a writing experience, or classify *eating utensils*, before setting the table for lunch.
2. If possible, let the child identify and label the base for sorting and classification.
3. Help the child check his classification.

Further Reference

Language 4.16

Sociology 7.21

Sociology

7.00   Goals in Sociology

7.10   Recalling Sequence of a Day's Activities

7.11   Self-Knowing: Photograph Recognition

7.12   Self-Valuing

7.13   Group Membership: School

7.14   Group Membership: Community

7.20   Holiday Craft Projects: Chart A

7.21   Craft Projects: Chart B

7.22   Woodworking

7.30   Art Experiences

7.00 GOALS IN SOCIOLOGY

Selected learnings in sociology stress such important features of school atmosphere, attitudes and procedures as:

1. Encouragement of child's autonomy and independence by honoring his right of choice or refusal.
2. Warm and respectful interactions with the young child convey affection, confidence in the child's ability to learn and expectations that he will freely invest himself in school experiences.
3. Preparing the classroom so that materials are arranged for easy access and maintenance, to encourage the child's selection and care of equipment and independent activity.
4. Valuing the child's uniqueness as a person by featuring evidence of his personal attributes including his name, photograph, voice, art work, preferences, and skill achievement.
5. Fostering the child's sense of membership in such groups as the family, the school and the community through his orientation to physical space and to human relationships. Orientation to physical space includes the child's finding his way around the school and the route to and from home. Human relationships include school and community roles and responsibilities.

Behavioral Goals

A. SELF-KNOWING

1. Children produce their full names and names of others.
2. Children recognize their own images in the mirror, on a photograph, slide, or videotape.
3. Children recognize their own voices on recorded tape.
4. Children recognize a description of their clothing and of some of their distinctive physical attributes.
5. Children state their birthdates, addresses, and telephone numbers.
6. Children write their names and recognize them.
7. Children recognize their own art and craft products.

B. SELF-VALUING

1. Children select their own activities.
2. Children volunteer for specific forms of activity.
3. Children refuse to engage in activity which does not interest them at the time.
4. Children undertake to solve problems that are within their capability.

5. Children use their skills to help others.
6. Children accept help when needed and refuse help otherwise.
7. Children express themselves in art work and in such expressive activities as music, dance, block building, and language.
8. Children show pride in their achievements and products.

C. GROUP MEMBERSHIP

1. Family
   a. Children name family members and their relationships.
   b. Children identify some attributes of family membership, such as adult responsibility for child welfare and responsibilities of individual family members.
2. Classroom
   a. Children contribute to and comply with classroom rules.
   b. Children participate in such forms of total group activity as games, music, or planning.
   c. Children recapitulate and anticipate the classroom schedule of activities in sequence.
3. School
   a. Children name their school and comply with school rules.
   b. Children find the way to their classrooms and other key locations in the school.
   c. Children name some key school personnel.
4. Community
   a. Children name their community and identify it as theirs.
   b. Children follow a route to and from home.
   c. Children participate in walks or trips to such major institutions in the community as stores, post office, churches.
   d. Children participate in craft activities.
   e. Children become aware of some cultural ideals of holiday celebrations through craft production.

7.10 RECALLING SEQUENCE OF A DAY'S ACTIVITIES
GROUP SIZE: ALL

Behavioral Goal

Children recapitulate and anticipate the classroom schedule of activities in sequence.

Procedure

1. At the end of the first day of school, group children for a brief discussion of the sequence of the day's activities.
2. Help children recall the activities by saying, "When you arrived, what did you play with? After playtime, we had a snack. What did we eat? After the snack, what did we do?" Keep the recapitulation brief and lively.
3. Repeat daily, gradually eliciting more detail.
4. Later, elicit a summary of the previous day's activities on arrival, as a basis for planning the current day's program.
5. Later, tape record the summary of a day's activities. Replay it the next day, for planning and comparison with current day's activities. See Lang. 4.11.

Further Reference

Language 4.11

7.11 SELF-KNOWING: PHOTOGRAPH RECOGNITION
GROUP SIZE: 1, ALL

Behavioral Goals

1. Children identify their photographs or assigned symbols, such as a decal, and associate such symbols with their written names.
2. Children move symbols of their identity, such as a photograph or decal, from the left to the right of their name cards.
3. Children contribute to and comply with class rules.

Procedure

Materials

Name cards	Wall chart
Camera	Film and flash bulbs
Set of decals	

1. Make necklace name tags for children to wear during early weeks of school.
2. Name chart:
    a. Place name cards written in standard manuscript on wall chart or on bulletin board.
    b. Show child his name card and tell him, "I'm going to take your picture to put here, next to your name." If a camera is not available, help child select a decal to be placed on a small card next to his name.
    c. Tell child, "Each day when you come to school, move your picture from *this* side of your name to the *other* side." Demonstrate by moving his picture from the left to the right of his name.
    d. After working with children individually, work with the total group. Direct their attention to the wall chart with children's names and pictures, and remind them to move their pictures daily.
    e. Use this procedure for taking attendance or for any other purpose.
3. Variation:
    a. Make a helper chart with name cards and illustrated job titles. Jobs may include watering plants, feeding animals, setting table, passing wastebasket, washing paint brushes, and sponging tables.
    b. Practice use of helper chart until most children know it well.
    c. Give children responsibility for following job chart.
    d. When children have learned to write their names, give them the

responsibility of preparing new helper charts requiring writing of names and job titles. See Lang. 4.22.

e.   As children grow more skillful, add more job titles to chart.

Further Reference

Language 4.22

7.12 SELF-VALUING

Behavioral Goals

1. Children select their own activities.
2. Children volunteer for specific forms of activity.
3. Children refuse to engage in activity which does not interest them at the time.
4. Children undertake to solve problems that are within their capability.
5. Children use their skills to help others.

Procedure

1. During the early weeks of school, as children adjust to the new environment of the school and classroom, feature the right of choice-making in the following ways:

   a. Organize equipment and materials to provide an uncluttered setting with 3 to 5 clearly defined interest centers, such as housekeeping, block area, easel with 4 colors of paint, and manipulative materials for table play.

   b. Invite a child to use the materials, helping him make a selection, as needed, by walking around the room with him, talking about the various materials available. Accept the child's decision to observe or to participate, while, at the same time, expanding his perception of the choices available. Repeat this procedure as child tires of an activity and appears slow to seek another item of interest.

   c. During the first few days of school, invite the child's escort (mother or close relative) to visit briefly to see the room and materials. If a child seems reluctant to remain without his escort, invite the escort to stay for several extended visits, gradually withdrawing from direct contact with the child to observing from a distance, to leaving the room briefly, and finally to leaving the building. Although each step in the adult withdrawal from the child's classroom is taken without fanfare, it is with the child's knowledge that school is for him, and his escort will eventually leave.

   d. As children engage in play activities, move about the room to talk to each individual child daily, in an easy, relaxed conversational style.

   e. When it is time to change the activity, advise each child individually of impending change of activity, thereby allowing him time to complete his play, construction, or art work. Usually 3 to 5 minutes is sufficient notice to provide time for the child to adjust himself to terminate the activity.

   f. When large group activities are initiated, such as music, accept children's participation in passive as well as active forms. Some children may observe at a distance initially; others may participate minimally within the group. For a child who actively refuses to join the group, offer another quiet activity such as looking at a book or crayoning.

g. As routines are introduced, allow children time to adjust to unfamiliar activities. Some children may take several weeks to begin to take on such classroom behaviors as *clean-up, hand-washing,* or even *eating* in school. Expectations for participation in routines may be conveyed by such comments and questions as: "Which area are you going to help clean up, the blocks or the table games?" Or, as the child manipulates a puzzle, "When you finish putting the puzzle away, join the children here at the piano." "Do you want this water cold or warm for washing your hands?" "You forgot to flush the toilet."

h. Demonstrate respect for individual differences in participating in routines:

(1) Ask a child to select his area for helping with the clean-up task.

(2) Help children structure the clean-up task so that it does not overwhelm them. This may include suggesting the order for replacing blocks on shelves, setting up "work" teams, assigning "jobs," or creating a game to facilitate completion of the procedure.

(3) Accept different levels of performance, as having 2 blocks replaced by 1 child compared to 20 replaced by another.

(4) Accept varying attention spans, as 1 child moving about the room from area to area during clean-up while others sustain involvement in one area. The child with the short attention span may be given a series of short tasks successively.

2. Respond to children's performance and verbalizations to communicate, valuing them as important individuals in interests, forms of expression, accomplishments, ideas and perceptions by such procedures and teaching strategies as:

a. Displaying children's work on bulletin boards, sometimes asking a child to select his own work for display, and other times putting up teacher selected work. Feature individual forms of expression, avoiding expectations for conformity.

b. Elicit verbal descriptions about children's art and craft work, without requiring standard forms of explanation; that is, vary the eliciting moves to conform with what the teacher knows about the individual child. Occasionally, tape record the child's descriptions of his art work, for repeated listening, or write or type them for story booklets to add to the library collection. See Lang. 4.10, 4.11, and 4.64, and Soc. 7.30.

c. Elicit increased detail about children's perceptions as they sponta-neously verbalize. When time is limited, plan with the child for a later time when the conversation may be continued.

d. Feature children's spontaneous chants by repeating them, and using them in the music program or at other appropriate times. See Music 3.11.

e. Exhibit children's science discoveries or investigations on special exhibit shelves or on a science table, labeling when appropriate, or tape recording children's reports for replay.

f. Photograph block structures for discussion and display before children are required to put them away. See Geog. 8.40 and 8.41.

g. Initiate or pursue discussions which feature individual preferences, such as favorite colors, food, and activities. See Math. 5.45 for some graphing procedures.

h. Feature each child's competencies in such routines as serving snacks, clean-up and clothing management, providing necessary help, not only by participation but also by illustrating procedures that lead to independence. For example, position a coat on the chair or floor so the child may don it without adult help.

i. Respect a child's periodic need for solitude, or physical affection or a moment of personal attention by responding to cues offered by the children.

Further Reference

Geography 8.40, 8.41

Language 4.10, 4.11, 4.64

Mathematics 5.45

Music 3.11

Sociology 7.30

7.13 GROUP MEMBERSHIP: SCHOOL

Behavioral Goals

1. Children indicate their sense of school group membership by:
   a. Responding appropriately to signals for change in behavior (for example, to discontinue play and to start to clean up);
   b. Complying with classroom rules; for example, in how, where, and when materials are to be used, and in sharing or taking turns;
   c. Offering to help other children or asking for other children's help (especially in the routines of clean-up, dressing, and undressing, and in social play situations).
2. Children verbalize their sense of school group membership by:
   a. Verbal references to "our class," "our school," "our children," and "our teacher";
   b. Use of names of other children and teacher;
   c. Contributing to classroom rule-making, or verbalizing rule knowledge.

Procedure

1. Teach children to change behavior to accord with classroom signals for change in behavior during transitions or activity change such as fire drill.
   a. *Warning or alerting signals* to anticipate transition or change in activity, such as "five-minute-notice" signal indicated by:
      Light flicks
      Bell ringing
      Piano chord
      Teacher chant, "Five more minutes to clean-up time"
      Repeat of signal to mark the beginning of change in behavior, or the transitional period.
   b. *Special signals* to communicate instant change in behavior, as for fire drills or to hear an announcement or to discuss a problem such as the high noise level of the group. Signal might be a bell tone or musical instrument used only for this signal, or turning out lights.
2. Teach children to comply with classroom rules, to cooperate, and coordinate behavior to accord with simple classroom rules.
   a. Communication of expectations:
      (1) For sharing use of materials by such comments as:
          "Susie wants a turn. Call her when you are finished."
          "Susie wants a turn. Will you finish soon so she may have a turn today?"
          "Find a place for the paste jar so you both can reach it without getting in each other's way."

(2) For care and use of materials; by such comments as:
"You forgot to put the puzzle into the puzzle rack, over here, like this."
"Here's a puzzle piece you missed when you put your puzzle away."
"There's a toy on the floor that doesn't belong there, Harry. "Can you find a safe place for it so it won't get stepped on and broken?"
"All the pieces of the game are here. You have taken excellent care of this game."

(3) Modeling rule and verbalizing, such as:
(a) Telling children, "When you are finished with the clay, roll it into a ball like this, before putting it back here in the crock. This way, the clay will stay moist, and not dry out so fast," while demonstrating the procedure.
(b) Teacher moves her picture from the left to the right of name on name chart, verbalizing, "I'm moving my picture from this left side of my name to this right side, to show that I'm in school today."

3. Teach children to help other children and ask other children to help, playing leader or follower in classroom group efforts during routines and helper jobs.
   a. Establish procedures for children to fill helper roles in the classroom, such as table setting, monitoring clean-up in a selected area of classroom, serving snacks, and holding door open for exit or entrance. This could include:
   (1) Helper charts that children can "read" to discover helper assignments each day;
   (2) Children's notation in some form that they have completed task;
   (3) Team assignments, or a leader and helper for each assignment;
   (4) Appointment of children to monitor materials use in specified interest areas.
   b. Communicate expectations that children will help each other by such comments as:
   "Susie, Barbara is very good with zippers. Why don't you ask her to help you with your coat while I get the paintings ready to go home?"
   "When you children are finished picking up these blocks, see if you can find someone who needs your help to finish his job."
   "John needs help in tying his shoes. Can anyone here help him?"

"Children, if you need help with zippers or boots, find a friend to help you."

    c. Direct attention to the benefits of cooperative participation within the context of routines by such comments as:

"You finished clean-up very fast because everybody helped. Now we have more time to play."

"When you help each other dress for outdoors it goes much faster. Nobody has to wait."

    d. Model the helper role as a cooperative group member, by such participation as:

      (1) Entering block area when the task of clean-up seems oppressive, and pitching in to help, with the comment, "You need all the help you can get with this big job, and I have a few moments" (teacher may select her share of the task or ask the children what they would like her to do);

      (2) Joining a group that is having difficulty washing down tables, and modeling the procedure for squeezing the sponge so it doesn't drip water all over the floor;

      (3) Responding to requests for help.

4. Teach children to make verbal references to group membership.

    a. Initiate discussions that feature "our class," or "our school," including such activities as:

      (1) Composing group stories about class activities for typing, duplicating, and tape recording;

      (2) Taking photographs of group engaged in class activities for posting or including in class book for library corner;

      (3) Suggesting musical activities and games that require use of names of class members, as "Jump to your name" (See Music 3.20);

      (4) Using name charts posted in class for recording such aspects as attendance, helper assignment, participation in interest centers, and children's learning interests;

      (5) Encouraging impromptu dramatizations by small groups with the rest of the class as audience;

      (6) Planning dramatizations or shows as entertainment for other class groups or family members;

      (7) Initiating group projects, such as cooking jello for dessert.

5. Teach children to contribute to classroom rule-making or verbalizing rule knowledge.

    a. Feature rules that children devise for classroom functioning. When children conflict, resolve the conflict by using a rule, such as "You shouldn't take a chair from somebody. You should get your own chair," or "That card is for the lotto game. It doesn't belong here."

  b. Identify confusions and conflicts that need some guiding rule, and discuss possible solutions; as when children's block buildings appear to be too close to each other, the teacher may anticipate the problem of accidental destruction and help to develop a rule for spacing with the children.

  c. Verbalize rules while modeling them.

Further Reference

Music 3.20

7.14 GROUP MEMBERSHIP: COMMUNITY
GROUP SIZE: 5, ALL

Behavioral Goals

1. Children participate in walks or trips to such major institutions in the community as stores, post office, churches, transportation terminals, library, museum, or theater.
2. Children name their community and some of its specific features.

Procedure

1. Identify children's needs or interests in acquiring information about major institutions in the community; for example, a visit to a pet shop or to a local zoo to obtain information needed prior to acquisition of a classroom pet. See Sci. 6.23 and Geog. 8.31.
2. Help children to clarify what information they are seeking and to focus on a few questions.
3. Plan the trip carefully so that it is a happy experience, with a good chance that children can acquire desired information.
4. Since young children are easily overstimulated by trips, limit trips in duration and purposes.
5. Plan short trips earlier in the year and reserve longer trips for later periods when children have the stamina required.
6. If possible, take along a camera, so that you will have photographs or slides or 8mm movie film to use in the classroom, to recapture features of the trip. See Soc. 7.12.
7. Use these photographs later to help children recall the trip, to name the institution visited, and to identify with the community.
8. Encourage children to tape record their trip experiences. See Lang. 4.11.
9. Produce duplicated booklets based on these experiences. See Lang. 4.64.

Further Reference

Language 4.11, 4.64

Science 6.23

Sociology 7.12

Geography 8.31

7.20 HOLIDAY CRAFT PROJECTS

Art and craft materials are expected to be made available for exploration and manipulation by children during most of the program. Craft activities are distinguished from art activities by the utilitarian nature of most craft projects. Craft projects are suggested as a means of heightening children's interest and enthusiasm for practicing use of key language and exploring the application of related learnings. Craft products are expected to reflect the individual choices of materials and production skills of the children.

To feature children's choices, avoid rigid adherence to a prescribed project and avoid adult directions that lead to making carbon copies of a model.

Behavioral Goals

1. Children participate in craft activities.
2. Children make craft products relating to holiday celebrations.
3. Children recognize and take pride in their achievements and products.
4. Children become aware of some cultural ideals of holiday celebrations through craft production.

CHART A: HOLIDAY CRAFT PROJECTS

Holiday Project	Learning Goal	Key Language	Materials
Columbus Day			
1. box-like boats for floating and making exhibits	*Math. 5.20* Shapes *Sci. 6.11* Experimenting with objects	rectangular solid (hull) triangle, rectangle (sail) float, sink	scissors paste, tape, stapler milk cartons styrofoam, cardboard paper, fabric enamel paint water
Halloween			
2. masks for dramatic play and music, cut-out, painted, crayoned, pasted	*Math. 5.20* Shapes *Sci. 6.10* Properties of objects *Lang. 4.10* Eliciting and extending *Cog. Skills 2.24* Patterning	circle, square, triangle rectangle, soft-hard rough-smooth scary, funny	scissors paste, tape, stapler construction paper, or paper bags string, yarn collage materials

Sociology 7.20

CHART A: *(continued)*

Holiday Project	Learning Goal	Key Language	Materials
3. Jack O'Lantern: Real pumpkins or child-made, for dramatic play, music or room decoration	*Math. 5.20* Shapes *Sci. 6.10, 6.11* Properties of objects *Lang. 4.10* Eliciting and extending *Math. 5.70, 5.71* Linear measurement	circle, square, triangle wet, dry, soft, stringy smooth shiny scary, funny	pumpkin, knife construction paper scissors gummed shapes cellophane paper stapler, tape
Thanksgiving 4. cookies, cooking and eating	*Math. 5.20* Shapes *Sci. 6.21* Transforming properties *Lang. 4.10, 4.13* Eliciting and extending—using precise language	spheres, rectangular solids circle, square, triangle, rectangle soft, smooth, powdery, wet dry, crisp, sticky, doughy	cookie ingredients, either mix or flour, sugar, flavoring, and other desired ingredients
5. placemats for party decoration	*Cog. Skills 2.24* Patterning, extending, and creating *Math. 5.20* Shapes	color names circle, square, triangle pattern names, such as red-red-blue-blue or circle-square	construction paper or oak tag gummed shapes or strips other collage materials sponge printing with water paint
6. indian headdress for dramatic play and music	*Math. 5.20* Shapes *Math. 5.70, 5.71* Linear measurement	triangle, rectangle, circle length, long, ruler tapemeasure pattern	tape measure strips of construction paper scissors, paste, tape feathers, collage materials
7. tomahawk	*Cog. Skills 2.22, 2.23, 2.24* Patterning	row, pattern weapon, warpath	oaktag, collage materials cardboard crayon, paper shapes, paste

CHART A: *(continued)*

Holiday Project	Learning Goal	Key Language	Materials
Chanukah– Christmas Gifts			
8. pencil holders	*Math. 5.11* Members of sets *Math. 5.20* Shapes *Sci. 6.10, 6.11* Properties of objects and experimenting *Cog. Skills 2.24* Patterning	cylinder, triangle, circle, square, rectangle color names patterns	cans, to be decorated with collage materials paint, sequins, shapes
9. wooden tie bars	*Soc. 7.22* Woodworking	smooth, saw, screw	wood, cup hooks, enamel paint sandpaper
10. picture frames	*Math. 5.70* Linear measurement	circular, rectangular, square measure, length, longer, shorter	cardboard, oaktag collage materials printing materials
11. vanity boxes	*Math. 5.20* Shapes *Sci. 6.10, 6.11* Properties of objects	rectangular solids	wood, cardboard, collage decorating materials paint
12. wooden pull-toy	*Math. 5.20* Shapes	wheels, round, roll rectangular solids	wheels, wood, string woodworking tools
13. gift wrap paper	*Cog. Skills 2.24* Patterning *Math. 5.20* Geometric shapes *Sci. 6.10* Properties of objects	patterns circle, square, triangle color names	potato prints sponges shapes collage materials tempera paint paste
14. tree decorations	*Math. 5.20* Shapes *Sci. 6.21* Transforming properties	rectangular solids balls, spheres, cones sticky, pasty, wet, moist, dry, hard, soft, powder	papier-mâché paint and paper cans, boxes cut paper styrofoam, cotton paste, scissors

CHART A: *(continued)*

Holiday Project	Learning Goal	Key Language	Materials
15. Room decorations, such as mobiles and paper chains	*Soc. 7.21* Mobiles *Cog. Skills 2.24* Patterning	color patterns	construction paper paste, scissors stapler
Presidents' Birthdays <u>Lincoln</u>			
16. top hats	*Lang. 4.90* Dramatization *Math. 5.20* Shapes *Math. 5.70, 5.71* Linear measurement	cylinder circle measure size	construction paper paste tapemeasure stapler
17. flag	*Cog. Skills 2.24* Patterning *Math. 5.20* Shapes *Lang. 4.90* Dramatization	stripes, stars alternating pattern rectangle color names	construction paper colored paper strips stars sticks paste, scissors
George Washington			
18. hatchet	*Math. 5.20* Shapes *Lang. 4.90* Dramatization *Sci. 6.11* Experimenting	rectangle rectangular solid	wood or heavy construction paper crayon paste stapler
19. three-cornered hats	*Math. 5.20* Shapes	triangle	construction paper paste, stapler
Valentine's Day 20. cards	*Math. 5.20* Shapes *Sci. 6.10, 6.11* Properties of objects *Lang. 4.90* Dramatization *Geog. 8.31* Trips	color names hearts friends mailbox, post office stamps poems, rhymes	paste, glue stapler, crayons, paints construction paper, scissors doilies: cotton, metallic paper, pipe cleaners, crepe paper, wax paper, tissue paper felt, needles, and yarn
21. mailbox	*Geog. 8.32* Movement of information	rectangular solid	carton, decorations

CHART A: *(continued)*

Holiday Project	Learning Goal	Key Language	Materials
Easter 22. baskets	*Math. 5.20* Shapes *Math. 5.70* Linear Measurement	rectangular solid	milk cartons oaktag, pipe cleaners decorative materials paste, stapler
23. bonnets	*Cog. Skills 2.24* Patterning *Lang. 4.90* Dramatization	spheres	paper plates, construction paper, collage materials doilies, styrofoam balls crepe paper, lace, net paste, stapler
24. dyeing eggs	*Sci. 6.10, 6.11, 6.21* Properties and transforming properties	crayon resist, color names water, change stencils smells	water, dye, vinegar, hard- boiled eggs, crayons

Further Reference

Cognitive Skills 2.24

Language 4.10, 4.13, 4.90

Mathematics 5.11, 5.20, 5.70, 5.71

Science 6.10, 6.11, 6.21

Sociology 7.22

Geography 8.31

CHART B: CRAFT PROJECTS

Project	Learning Goals	Key Language		Materials
1. collage: single purpose a. shape	*Sci. 6.40* Sorting on a specified base *Math. 5.20* Geometric shapes	circle triangle make a pattern copy a pattern color names round	square rectangle corners	a. construction paper, gummed shapes, toothpicks, washers, Mason jar rings, yarn, pipe cleaners, paper strips, paste, stapler
b. texture: emphasize contrasting tactile properties	*Sci. 6.10 and 6.11* Properties of objects *Math. 5.11* Members of sets	hard-soft smooth-rough rigid-flexible flat-curved shiny-dull hollow-solid		b. construction paper, glue, paste, stapler or tape; assorted materials such as cotton, cork, aluminum foil, yarn, wire, wood, rubber, buttons, straws
c. order by length: make a row of different kinds of flowers on a baseline, ordered from tallest to shortest	*Math. 5.60* Ordering by length *Sci. 6.11* Properties of objects	tallest-shortest longest color names soft-smooth stem petal flower leaf		c. construction paper with baseline marked, varying lengths of pipe cleaners, pop sticks, strips of paper for flower stems; gummed circles, crepe paper, cotton, ribbon, felt, buttons, tissue paper for flowers
d. number	*Math. 5.42* Create a set to match a given number *Math. 5.50* Associate numerals with number of objects in a set	number names object labels color labels same number		d. assorted collage materials, paper, paste, scissors, numeral stamps, crayons
e. size: big-little long-short	*Lang. 4.13* Precise vocabulary *Sci. 6.10* Properties of objects *Math. 5.11* Members of sets	big-little name labels		e. 2 sizes of big and little selected materials such as buttons, cotton balls, cardboard discs; 2 lengths of selected materials, such as wooden sticks, pipe cleaners, paper strips

CHART B: *(continued)*

Project	Learning Goals	Key Language	Materials
f. position. collage featuring: up above-down below, land or sea, city or country	*Geog. 8.10* Positional terms *Math. 5.20* Geometric shapes	up above-down below over under on top of underneath circle triangle	f. construction paper with horizontal line drawn, paste, crayons *sea:* boat decals or cut-outs, fish decals or cut-outs, bird decals or cut-outs, cotton, stars, white and yellow circles *city:* decals or picture clippings of trucks, planes, cars, subway, urban streets, people, buildings, cotton, felt, copper wire *country:* decals or picture clippings of farm animals, trees, flowers, vegetables, rocks, worms, grass, cotton, birds
2. single-purpose books			paper, paste, tape, stapler
a. color books	*Lang. 4.13* Precise vocabulary	color names	a. assorted materials and objects of desired colors
b. shape books	*Math. 5.20* Shapes	circle triangle rectangle	b. hole punch, circles, triangles, squares of paper, fabric, cardboard, stencils of shapes
c. number books	*Math. 5.50* Numerals	number names	c. assorted objects of various sizes, such as macaroni, buttons, pipe cleaners, decals, cork, numeral stamps, paste
d. pattern books	*Lang. 4.13* Precise vocabulary	color names object labels	d. objects suitable for printing with paint, such as a plastic fork, cork or wooden spool, plastic bottle cap, potatoes cut for printing, sponge squares, paint and paper

CHART B: *(continued)*

Project	Learning Goals	Key Language	Materials
e. classification books (may be combined with number books)	*Math. 5.11* Members of sets *Sci. 6.40* Sorting and classifying	farm animals pets growing things tools people vehicles toys	e. assortment of decals or cut-outs of desired class mixed with other pictures, picture magazines, paper and paste
3. mobiles: single purpose			
a. number mobiles	*Math. 5.42* Counting	number names "a-three-mobile"	a. wire hanger, pieces of string, buttons, feathers, springs, beads, paper circles
b. shape mobiles	*Math. 5.20* Shapes	circle square triangle rectangle spheres or balls rectangular solids cones	b. wire hanger, pieces of string, tape, scissors varied balls: styrofoam, rubber ping-pong small boxes, precut shapes, pipe cleaners
c. color mobiles	*Lang. 4.13* Precise vocabulary	color names object names	c. wire hanger, pieces of string, tape, solid color objects, pictures
4. decorative frames for children's artwork	*Math. 5.70* Arbitrary linear measure *Cog. Skills 2.24* Children extend and create patterns *Cog. Skills 2.20* Positional terms	measure count inch ruler length width height tall longer shorter yardstick edge top side bottom left-right read the ruler read the pattern	mounting strips of oaktag, ribbon, paper; scissors, paste, tape, stapler; assorted materials for decorating frame, such as buttons, macaroni, gummed shapes, pipe cleaners, paste, and stapler; cork circles or strips; paper clips, rubber bands
5. necklaces, bracelets, belts; objects on a string	*Cog. Skills 2.24* Children extend and create patterns *Math. 5.71* Teacher modeling of measurement	alternating pattern read the pattern a red-red-blue pattern a button-button-bead-bead pattern color names shape names object names	strings for necklaces, bracelets, belts, tape measures; assorted materials for stringing, such as beads, macaroni—white or dyed, cork balls, buttons, lace, fabric

CHART B: *(continued)*

Project	Learning Goals	Key Language	Materials
6. decorative placemats, wrapping paper, book covers, and bulletin board hangings	*Cog. Skills 2.24* Creating and copying patterns *Math. 5.20* Shapes *Math. 5.11* Members of sets *Sci. 6.10, 6.11* Properties of objects	a long-short pattern a big-little pattern a macaroni-bean pattern a color pattern, red-red-blue, red-red-blue a shape pattern, fork-fork-circle-fork-fork-circle	paste, glue, tape, stapler, paper, cardboard, oaktag pasted patterns: macaroni and beans, cranberries and popcorn, buttons and bows printed patterns: potatoes cut for printing, plastic forks, bottle caps, sponge squares; collections of materials contrasting one property
7. complete-it books	*Cog. Skills 2.24* Completing and extending patterns	fill in the missing item read the pattern and find the missing part make a pattern, but leave one part out	booklets with series of incomplete patterns, of shapes or colors, having items missing; blank booklets, with lines drawn on each page; gummed shapes
8. number stick	*Math. 5.50* Numerals	count number names number stick	tongue depressors, beans, beads, glue, paste

7.22 WOODWORKING
GROUP SIZE: 1, 2

Behavioral Goals

1. Children recognize and take pride in their achievements and products.
2. Children undertake to solve problems.
3. Children participate in craft activities to make products relating to holiday celebrations.

Procedure

Materials

Basic:

Wood—soft pine:	4 foot lengths	Vise
	3 foot lengths	Roofing nails: 1, 1-1/2, 2 inch
	1/4, 1/2, 3/8	Sandpaper: coarse, medium, fine
	inch thick	Enamel paint, brush, turpentine,
Saw, 16 inch crosscut		or water paint and shellac
Hammer, 13 oz. claw		Ruler, pencil

Auxiliary:

Wooden dowels:	3 feet long	Cork balls
	1/8, 1/4, 1/2, 1	Tongue depressors
	inch diameter	Fabric
Hand drill and set of drill bits		Styrofoam
Screws		Pipe cleaners
Screwdriver, 3 and 4 inch		Copper wire
Pliers		String
Wooden wheels, assorted sizes		Bells
		Cup hooks

1. Initiate experiences with wood and woodworking tools primarily for exploration and manipulation. Help children discover what tools can do to wood. See Sci. 6.10, 6.11, and 6.21.
2. Accept completed products in the beginning, consisting only of a piece of wood sawed by the child, or a nail hammered into a piece of wood.
3. Introduce key language in context, as children manipulate the tools and materials. See Lang. 4.11.
4. Adjust children's position so that they saw comfortably at a downward angle.
5. Check vise to make sure wood is securely held.
6. Suggest rhythmic motion in sawing by chanting, "Easy does it. Easy does it."
7. Make a notch with the saw to help the child begin to saw through the the wood.
8. For young children, help to start hammering a nail either by making a shallow hole with him or for him, or starting the nail for him.
9. Gradually introduce more tools and supplementary materials listed above.
10. Measurement: Help children to use arbitrary and standard forms of measurement, when their projects require it. See Math. 5.70 and 5.71.
11. Project selection: Gradually, as children develop skill in woodworking, help them to select more interesting projects. Select from such projects as:

Boat	Belt rack
Car	Puppet stage
Truck	Decorative storage boxes
Train	Garage
Plane	Doll bed
Pull toys	Napkin box
Picture frame	Toy shelf
Tie bar	

12. Encourage children to find projects which result in products usable in classroom play, such as a miniature garage for cars or a doll bed.
13. Techniques of finishing wood:
    a. Sanding: Provide coarse, medium, and fine grades of sandpaper
    b. Paint: Provide enamel paint or water paint, followed by shellac
    c. Decoration: Provide wallpaper samples and paste, self-adhesive plastic, crayons, or other forms of decoration

Key Language

Includes properties of objects, positional terms, geometric shapes, color names, object labels, descriptive terms, such as:

Hard-soft	Rough-smooth
Long-short	Longer-shorter
Thick-thin	Thicker-thinner
Narrow-narrower	Round, square, flat
Rectangular, solid	Ball, sphere
Measure	Top-bottom
Under-over	Next to, beside
Sawdust	Names of tools, materials, processes, and products

Further Reference

Language 4.11

Mathematics 5.70, 5.71

Science 6.10, 6.11, 6.21

Geography 8.41

7.30 ART EXPERIENCES
GROUP SIZE: 1, 2, 5

Behavioral Goals

1. Children express themselves in art work and in such expressive activities as music, dance, block building, and language.
2. Children take pride in their achievements and products.

Procedure

Materials

Easel	Tempera paint
Brush	Newsprint
Finger paint	Clay
Clay boards	Construction paper
Pastels	Chalk
Crayons	Pencils
Various kinds of paper	Scissors

Collage materials

1. Offer daily choices among art experiences.
2. Set up a work center for art materials.
3. Help children develop clear rules for care and clean-up of materials.
4. Give children as much independence as they can handle in exploring art materials.
5. Let children solve problems whenever possible.
6. Share with children the joy of activity in art work.
7. If comments on children's products seem indicated, use objective statements such as:

   "You worked a long time."

   "You enjoyed your work."

   "You used a lot of brown."

   "Your lines are mostly round."

   "It's a big picture."

"I watched you painting."

"This is your second painting today."

8. Refrain from teaching perspective or otherwise intervening in the child's expressive activity.

9. If child seeks help of a factual nature, such as "How can I make purple paint?" or "What does a horse look like?" respond with information orally, or from models, books, and dictionaries.

10. If child requests help in choosing a subject or in finding a way to represent an object, refrain from doing his work for him, but help him, through conversation, or in other ways, to get started. For example, if child asks help to paint a lunar module, refer him to photographs, and help him to focus on some key features so he can get started in his art activity.

11. If child chooses to represent a subject beyond his ability, redirect him to a subject within his ability, such as a purely expressive painting of a nonrepresentational type. Use such verbal suggestions as, "Paint a picture to show how you feel. Make an interesting design. Use the color you like best. How many colors would you like to use?"

12. If child expresses frustration in working with material, offer help to improve techniques in use of material, or offer substitute material. For example, add water to dry clay, discard muddy-colored paint and replace with clear colors, substitute heavy paper for paper too thin for the project.

13. Accept child's completed work without suggesting changes or addition of detail and without adverse comments.

14. Display children's art work impartially, valuing each product.

15. Keep a folder for each child's art work, to maintain a school collection to share with parents and visitors.

16. Send home samples of children's art work, either weekly or monthly.

Geography

8.00   Goals in Geography
8.01   Some Basic Ideas about Geographical Study
8.10   Orientation in Space: Obstacle Game
8.20   Responding to and Using Directional Terms of Right-Left
8.30   Walk Inside School Building
8.31   Neighborhood Walk
8.32   Trips Requiring Transportation
8.40   Representing a Street Using a Strip of Paper
8.41   Representing Physical Space with Physical Objects

8.00 GOALS IN GEOGRAPHY

Geographical study is concerned with attributes of the physical environment and the process of changes in the environment. These changes result from changes in such factors as population, industrial development, and political control.

Children develop geographical concepts as they move and interact within physical spaces, distinguishing details and features of their neighborhood in relation to themselves.

Initial learnings concentrate on the child's self-orientation, directionality, identification of such physical urban features as streets, sidewalks, buildings, vehicles, movements of people and objects, some primary relationships among these features, and changes that can be observed.

Behavioral Goals

1. Children move in space avoiding collision with people and things.
2. Children move on a designated path from its beginning to its end.
3. Children demonstrate directionality by identifying right and left parts of the body and movement to the right and left.
4. Children identify such features of a specific physical environment as:
    a. Land surface use in streets adjacent to school, such as buildings, stores, parks, vacant lots;
    b. Use of buildings as for residential, educational or commercial use;
    c. Movement of people, vehicles and animals on sidewalks and streets;
    d. Movement of information through the mail and telephones;
    e. Children's routes to school, stores, churches, subway, parks.
5. Children represent features of physical space by physical objects, such as blocks.
6. Children make appropriate physical responses to such forms of spatial relationships as: in front of-behind, first-last, over-under, inside-outside, forward-backward, left-right.
7. Children demonstrate directionality by identifying right and left sides of a flat surface such as a sheet of paper.

8.01 SOME BASIC IDEAS ABOUT GEOGRAPHICAL STUDY

Geography is a study of the processes by which physical and spatial aspects of the environment are transformed. Essentially, geography is a study of the changes in our physical environment and, especially, of the interrelatedness of change; that is, change in any physical aspect tends to produce changes in all other aspects, physical and often nonphysical.

Five interdependent dimensions of geographical space follow:
1. The population and its attributes, such as extent of population crowding and educational and income levels.
2. The environmental attributes, such as weather and climate, proximity to other population centers.
3. The organizational aspects, including economic, political, and other organizational institutions.
4. The social-psychological aspect, or the relationships of social groups to each other.
5. The technological aspect, or the level and extent of mechanization.

All of these dimensions are interrelated and affect each other. A change in any one dimension will be accompanied by changes in the other aspects.

The organization of an urban geographical system has the five following components:

1. *Movements* refer to movements of people, things or ideas from one place to another. For example, people move from place to place, and so do cars and telephone messages. The term *desire-lines* is used to identify the connection between the points where movements originate and terminate. For example, there are innumerable desire-lines from Times Square to all corners of New York City.
2. *Channels* refers to the paths that movements take. For example, streets, bridges, elevators, stairs, hallways and highways are all channels. So are telephone lines, telegraph lines, cables, the post office system, air routes, and so forth.
3. *Nodes* are points where channels intersect, such as street intersections.
4. *Hierarchies* refer to the scale of complexity of nodal composition. For example, an intersection in a city residential area might have one newsstand. In contrast, at Times Square in Manhattan, there are multiple uses of the same site for such varied purposes as residential, commercial, professional, industrial, retail, entertainment, and transportation. This also suggests the contrast of a two-street intersection and a multiple-artery intersection.

5. *Surfaces* refer to all the physical aspects of space. Surface use, for example, may range from park space reserved for recreational use to high-rise buildings incorporating multiple space use, as residential, commercial, and recreational.

8.10 ORIENTATION IN SPACE: OBSTACLE GAME
GROUP SIZE: 5, ALL

Behavioral Goals

1. Children move in space avoiding collision with people and things.
2. Children respond physically to verbal instructions using terms of spatial relationship and directionality.
3. Children verbalize terms of spatial relationship, labeling actions.

Procedure

Materials

Select from:

Chalked lines on playground pavement or classroom floor

Walking boards

Sawhorse

Other similar objects

1. Invite children to help you set up an obstacle path, either on the playground or in the classroom. The path may be two chalked parallel lines two feet apart, or walking boards or any other way to delineate a straight, narrow path. Initially, place no obstacles on the path. Gradually, add various obstacles to complicate the game.

Key Language

In front of	Behind
First	Last
Over	Under
Inside	Outside
Forward	Backward
Around	

2. Game: Path to Home
    a. Place a large object such as box or chair at one end of the path, designating it as *home*. Model walking on the path, saying, "In this game, we have to get to home. But we must stay on the path until we touch home."

197

    b.   Ask children to walk the path, in turn.

    c.   Add one obstacle and say, "Here is an obstacle. How can you reach home now? Remember, in this game you must stay on the path."

    d.   Encourage the children to find a way home.

    e.   Elicit from children how they reach home, comparing actions. Supply key language, such as, "Derrick climbed over the box and Sharon walked around it."

3. Vary obstacles as follows:

    a.   Raise walking board slightly, resting it on large blocks.

    b.   Place a board across the path, first low, to be stepped over, then high, to crawl under.

    c.   Place pile of objects on the middle of the path.

Key Language

Step up

Step down

Step over

Crawl under

Go around

4. Encourage the children to invent new obstacles and then figure out appropriate instructions.

Further Variations

Select a *caller*, who instructs each person how to walk down the path. Model caller role, saying, "John, walk down the path, step up, step down, touch home. Susan, walk down the path, jump over the block, touch home."

8.20 RESPONDING TO AND USING DIRECTIONAL TERMS OF RIGHT—LEFT

GROUP SIZE: ALL

Behavioral Goals

1. Children demonstrate directionality (right-left) by movement and song.
2. Children demonstrate directionality by identifying right and left parts of the body.

Procedure

Materials

Loops of jersey, yarn, pipe cleaners, crepe paper or gummed shapes
Music for "Looby-Loo" or "Hokey-Pokey"
Drum

1. Each day as children enter, mark each child's right side with a marker, such as a loop on the right wrist, or a sticker on the right hand. Say, "This marks your right side."
2. Musical game
   a. Line up children single file, for game, as in a marching line.
   b. Sing "Looby-Loo," modeling actions of song. Help children remember right and left parts of body to conform to song, reminding them of the markers, as needed.

Variations

1. Hold a drum and face a marching line of children. Ask children to march past you striking with their right hand, chanting, "Right! Right!"
2. Initiate "Simon Says," emphasizing right and left, such as, "Simon says stamp your right foot." Later, select a child as leader.

8.30 WALK INSIDE SCHOOL BUILDING
GROUP SIZE: ALL

Behavioral Goal

Children identify key locations and pathways inside the school building.

Procedure

1. Briefly discuss with children the important locations in the building. Say, "We are in the prekindergarten (kindergarten) classroom in P.S._____. There are many other classrooms and other important rooms here. Let's go exploring."
2. Ask children to take partners. See Math. 5.10 for pairing.
3. As group walks around building, emphasize key aspects of the building, such as:
    a. Halls and stairways: pathways that lead from one part of building to another;
    b. Offices: rooms where adults work;
    c. Classrooms: rooms for children and teachers;
    d. Auditorium: room for many classes to meet for a special reason;
    e. Cafeteria: eating room.
4. Include increasing detail of observation in subsequent walks within school building. Encourage children to label additional rooms and spaces.

Further Reference

Mathematics 5.10

8.31 NEIGHBORHOOD WALK
GROUP SIZE: 5, ALL

Behavioral Goals

1. Children identify some features of a specific physical environment, such as sidewalks.
2. Children move on a designated path from its beginning to its end.

Procedure

1. Prepare group for walk by discussing the purpose of the trip, which may be:
   a. To walk completely around the school block, without crossing streets, to see where the path ends;
   b. To walk a designated path on named streets to a specified store, to make a specified purchase, and to return to school by the same path.
2. Ask children to select partners. See Math. 5.10 for pairing.
3. Develop a chant, as you walk, singing, "We walk *only* on the sidewalk," in a rhythmic, simple chant.
4. On return to school, ask group to recall the trip, the route, the purpose, the chant, and the *result*. The result might be that a pumpkin was purchased, or, if the walk was around the block, that the path ended exactly where it started.
5. Supply verbal labels freely.

Key Language

Street	Mailbox
Sidewalk	Hydrants
Traffic light	Store window
Buildings	Intersection or corner
Curb	

Variations in Purpose of Walk

1. Note movement and path of animate and inanimate objects (for example, people and animals versus cars, trucks, bicycles, motorcycles).
2. Note land surface use in streets adjacent to school, such as parks, buildings, stores, vacant lots, gas stations, and firehouses.

3. Note different uses of buildings, such as residential, educational, religious, and recreational.
4. Note movement of information, such as written information via letters, mailbox, mailman, post office, stamps, or verbal information via telephone, intercom systems, or public address systems.
5. Note types of stores in the community, such as food stores, clothes cleaners, shoe repair shops, clothing shops, restaurants, stationery stores, and five-and-dime stores.
6. Note variations in dwellings, such as high-rise apartment houses, low-rise multiple dwellings, and single-family houses.

Further Reference

Math 5.10

8.40 REPRESENTING A STREET USING A STRIP OF PAPER
GROUP SIZE: 1, 2, 5

Behavioral Goals

1. Children represent features of physical space by physical objects.
2. Children narrate classroom experiences.
3. Children read and write sentences and stories.

Procedure

Materials

Blocks

Strip of paper

Puppets

Block accessories such as miniature vehicles, animals and people, and floor tiles

1. Introduce activity following a great deal of children's voluntary manipulation and construction with blocks.
2. Initiate informal discussion with children in block play about recent walk to the store, or around the block, recalling physical features noted, such as streets, sidewalks, vehicles, animals, and people.
3. Offer a strip of paper to be a street and suggest to children that they put appropriate objects on street such as vehicles, with block construction of any type children choose.
4. After children make their construction, discuss it with them. Encourage labeling and differentiating of objects and use of physical space, such as street, sidewalk, curb, intersection and names of different vehicles and buildings.
5. After a later walk, help children distinguish between *street* and *sidewalk* and suggest they find a way to build a sidewalk next to the paper street, if they desire.
6. Later, ask children to note further features of the streets, such as mailboxes, traffic and street signs, traffic lights, fire hydrants, garbage cans, and specific types of delivery trucks.
7. Later, initiate informal discussions with block builders before they begin to build. Encourage them to plan a construction related to their gathering of information about physical features of the neighborhood. Later, recall the plans with the children, comparing plans to completed construction.
8. Once the group has completed a construction that was planned, photograph the construction and the builders.

9. Use photographs as the focus of a very simple story which you help children write. Add story to class library. See Lang. 4.64.

10. Read this booklet to the class and encourage children who participate in the project to "read" the booklet, to feature their competence and accomplishment. See Lang. 4.63

Further Reference

Language 4.63, 4.64

8.41 REPRESENTING PHYSICAL SPACE WITH PHYSICAL OBJECTS
GROUP SIZE: 2, 5

Behavioral Goals

1. Children identify features of physical environment such as land surface use and use of buildings.
2. Children represent features of physical space by physical objects, using terms of spatial relationship, such as *next to, above, below, behind, inside, outside, up, down.*

Procedure

Materials

Blocks

Block accessories

Strip of paper

Props as needed

1. Offer block accessories and strip of paper to block builders. Suggest planning a construction based on a recent walk.
2. Stress terms of spatial relationship, using them conversationally in context while planning with children. For example, "What are you going to build next to the school building? You parked your car behind his truck." See Lang. 4.10 and Geog. 8.10.
3. Help children make finer distinctions among physical characteristics of space. This includes curbs between streets and sidewalks, size of buildings, and any special features of the immediate area, such as constructions, or reconstruction, sidewalk obstructions, or street detours.
4. Later, after a number of walks to different stores, help interested children recall details concerning different stores nearby, for representation in the block construction. See Econ. 9.10.
5. Older or more mature children may want store signs, street signs, and other written posters. Help interested children to write, or write it for them. See Lang. 4.22.
6. Possible lines of interest children may want to pursue in their block representation include bridges, tunnels, elevators, airplanes and airports, a specific type of store or service, such as a laundromat, the subway, or the post office. As the children become interested in specific features of the environment, plan trips to provide first-hand information and experience.

Geography 8.41

Further Reference
Language 4.10, 4.22
Geography 8.10
Economics 9.10

Economics

9.00   Goals in Economics
9.10   Making Purchases in a Store
9.11   Role-Playing Buying and Selling
9.12   Making Purchases in a Store and Finding Desired Items
9.13   Role-Playing Buying and Selling and Grouping Items
9.14   Role-Playing Store Jobs

9.00 GOALS IN ECONOMICS

Children experience early many aspects of our economic system, particularly buying and selling in stores, various forms of service such as transportion, personal or health services, and some forms of production, such as building construction and renovation. Most forms of agricultural and industrial production are not available for urban children's first-hand experiencing. Therefore, the beginning learnings in economics have been confined to those common aspects of urban living with which most children have considerable early experience.

The design of the economics program moves in a circular fashion from first-hand group experiences, to playful dramatics, to structured dramatizations and forms of practice activities, back to first-hand experiences. Teaching suggestions offer many opportunities for *vocabulary-building* and for practice in using *forms* of *standard English*. Classification skills are featured in various forms of play and structure situations, as in differentiating food categories.

Behavioral Goals

1. Children use money to make a purchase (that is, exchange money for goods).
2. Children ask the price of things they buy.
3. Children ask for change when the money they offer to make a purchase is more than the price of the goods.
4. Children identify and differentiate denominations of coins and bills.
5. Children offer the exact amount of money when making small purchases requiring a nickel, a dime, a quarter, or several pennies.
6. Children differentiate buyers from sellers in a store.
7. Children name jobs in which people earn money, such as cashier, television repairman, house painter, plumber, salesman, building superintendent, janitor, barber, taxi driver, bus driver, subway trainmen, gas station attendant, teacher, doctor, dentist, and nurse.
8. Children differentiate school days from holidays and nonschool days and compare school days with days on which stores and other businesses do not operate.
9. Children demonstrate through creative dramatization and dramatic play that workers have hours of work and hours when they do not work.
10. Children differentiate specialized jobs within a store, to include such personnel as the manager, the cashier, and the store clerk.
11. Children demonstrate classification skills, in store play, dramatizations, and structured situations.

9.10 MAKING PURCHASES IN A STORE
GROUP SIZE: 5, ALL

Behavioral Goals

1. Children use money to make a purchase.
2. Children differentiate buyers from sellers in a store.
3. Children name some retail businesses in the community.

Procedure

Materials

Money in change (pennies, nickels, dimes, quarters)

Numeral and letter stamps and stamp pad

Pencils and paper

1. Plan a trip to a store to purchase a required item for a classroom activity, such as: a Halloween pumpkin, Jello, cranberries, assorted fruit, food for class pet, or seeds.
2. On the way to the store, discuss the type of stores observed, such as grocery store, clothing store, florist, or pet shop. Emphasize the various kinds of stores to alert children to the choices available in making purchases. Also, during the walk, emphasize geographic learning as per Geog. 8.31.
3. In the store, feature the act of exchange of goods for money by such statements as, "I am giving the storekeeper the money, and he is giving us the seeds. We are buying the seeds. He is selling us the seeds. We exchange money for seeds."
4. Plan several buying trips, if possible, to alert children to store size and variety of goods sold. For example, make a purchase in a supermarket, then in a produce store. Or go to a five-and-dime store after purchasing an item at a small dry goods store.
5. Follow trips with suggestions and props for store play in class. See Econ. 9.11 for materials and procedures for store play.

Further Reference

Geography 8.31

Economics 9.11

9.11 ROLE-PLAYING BUYING AND SELLING
GROUP SIZE: 2, 5, ALL

Behavioral Goals

1. Children role-play making purchases with money.
2. Children differentiate roles of buyers from sellers.
3. Children write numerals, words, and sentences.

Procedure

Materials

Props to encourage and stimulate dramatic play about buying and selling in stores, such as:

Toy money	Cash register
Dress-up clothes	Empty food cartons
Paper bags	Pocket books
Wallets	Coats and hats
Open-closed sign	Scale

Table, to be used as a store counter

1. Invite children to use this activity play center in any way they like.
2. Later, participate with children playing in this activity center. See Lang. 4.10 for eliciting language.
   a. Play the role of buyer and demonstrate the behavior and verbalization related to buying such as:

   "I want to buy a carton of milk. Do you have any milk? How much does it cost?"

   "Can you put my meat in a bag so I can carry it home?"

   "Don't I get any change? I gave you a five-dollar bill."

   "Can you deliver my groceries? Here's my address."

   "I ordered two cartons of milk but I only got one carton. Do you have another one?"

   "I want to buy some fresh milk tomorrow morning. What time does this store open?"

   "Yesterday, your store was closed. Why was it closed?"

"I want five pounds of potatoes and two dozen eggs."

"I see you have a special on chocolate pudding. If you have any left, I want to buy a lot—I'd like five boxes."

b. Play the role of seller, to demonstrate the behavior of the salesclerk or checker, using such verbalizations as:

"You ordered two quarts of milk. That will be 50 cents."

"You forgot your change. Here's your change."

"Do you want me to put your groceries in a bag?"

"We have a special sale on candy. Would you like to buy some?"

"I'm sorry; we don't have any bread left."

"You'd better hurry. Our store closes at six o'clock."

"Did you buy enough milk? This store will be closed tomorrow, because it will be Sunday."

"Sorry we can't deliver your groceries because our delivery boy is sick today."

"I'm sorry, you'll have to wait a few minutes until I take care of this man, who is ahead of you."

"I almost forgot to ring up this sale on my cash register."

3. Later, ask children to describe their store play activity, asking leading questions, if necessary, about money, prices, arrangements of merchandise, employees in the store, roles played, wages and hours of store employees.

4. Later, direct a simple buying-selling operation. See Lang. 4.90 for creative dramatization.
   a. Appoint or ask for a volunteer salesclerk.
   b. Distribute play money to children, such as paper or plastic discs to represent pennies, one to a child; or use toy money.
   c. Determine the item to be purchased. It may be some new collage material or a special treat, such as raisins.
   d. Explain that the store will open when the *open* sign is put up by the salesclerk, and that each child is entitled to buy one item with his "penny."
   e. Observe the selling operation, and let children take as much responsibility as they can handle.

5. Later, direct a more complex buying-selling operation, permitting choice of items to be purchased and choice of number of items to be purchased, depending on progress in mathematical learning. Suggest

more variety of store employee roles to be played, in addition to salesclerk and cashier, such as manager, wrapper, and store cleaner. Suggest or elicit additional needs for reading and writing.

Further Reference

Language 4.10, 4.90

9.12 MAKING PURCHASES IN A STORE AND FINDING DESIRED ITEMS
GROUP SIZE: 5, ALL

Behavioral Goals

1. Children demonstrate classification skills.
2. Children ask prices.
3. Children use money to make a purchase and ask for change.

Procedure

Materials

Money in coins and dollar bills

1. Plan a trip to the store to purchase a list of items; for example, the ingredients to make playdough or to bake a cake. Try to plan such a trip at a time when the store is least likely to be crowded.
2. Read the grocery list to the group and explain that when they get to the store, children will be asked to find one of the items on the list.
3. In the store, make up small teams of children to locate items on the list. Offer clues as needed, such as, "Where do you think the butter might be? Look for a place where they keep things cold."
4. At the check-out counter, give each child money to pay for his item, reminding him to ask the price and to ask for change.
5. Back in the classroom, try to elicit from children the item they located, the location in the store where the item was found, the price, and whether they received change.
6. Use the story about a trip like this for a duplicated booklet, as suggested in Lang. 4.64.

Further Reference

Language 4.64

9.13 ROLE-PLAYING BUYING AND SELLING AND GROUPING ITEMS
GROUP SIZE: 2, 5, ALL

Behavioral Goals

1. Children differentiate buyers from sellers.
2. Children demonstrate classification skills.

Procedure

Materials

A store play activity center with such props as:

"Shelves" made of large paper cartons

Empty food cartons	Number and letter stamps
Cash register	Stamp pad
Paper	Pencils
Price tags	Signs
Scale	Bags

1. Ask children to bring empty food containers from home to "stock" the store.
2. As stock accumulates and is used by children, play role of buyer and demand more than one box of a particular food, emphasizing the difficulty of finding it when items are not classified. Let children try to solve the problem.
3. If children do not initiate grouping items together that belong together, initiate this task. Say, "Could you put all the coffee cans on this shelf and the milk cartons on another shelf?"
4. Give children the responsibility of sorting the cartons, but observe their progress. Participate, if you think it necessary, offering suggestions, such as, "This isn't a coffee can. It doesn't belong with the coffee. It's a cereal box. Where should we put the cereal boxes?"
5. Accept children's classifications wherever there is any clear base for sorting.
6. Encourage writing of signs, to keep sorting operations clear. See Lang. 4.22.
7. Follow sorting and classifying activities as in Sci. 6.40.

Further Reference

Language 4.22

Science 6.40

9.14 ROLE-PLAYING STORE JOBS
GROUP SIZE: 5, ALL

Behavioral Goal

Children differentiate jobs in the store such as cashier, stock clerk, butcher, manager, produce clerk.

Procedure

Materials

Props for store play

Number and letter stamps

Additional items, such as:

Man's white shirt	Paper
Paper overseas cap	Crayons
Pencils	Tape or stapler

1. Plan for a trip to a supermarket to make some needed purchase, and to find out what jobs people do in the store.
2. Alert children in the store to the store employees and to the tasks they are performing. Say, "Here is the produce clerk. He takes care of the fruits and vegetables." Help children note such features as refrigerated food shelves or cases, price stamps, magic markers or crayons to write prices, scales, paper bags, tape or staplers to seal bags, cash register or adding machines, paper tapes or cash receipts, moving belts on counters, market baskets, or other tools and machines. Help children note which store employees use any of these items.
3. Suggest store play in classroom, on days following trip, by providing the materials listed above, and inviting children to select a store play role. Participate in a minor role, such as customer, to help develop the play sequences.
4. Help children recall observations they made on the trip, especially the tasks they saw store employees performing. If necessary, suggest use of number and letter stamps, pencils, crayons, and magic markers to write prices and signs.

Variations

1. Take a major role in store play, such as the manager, and direct the tasks of the "store" employees.

2. Help children frame questions for a follow-up trip to the supermarket. For example, "Who brought out the produce? Who packed the groceries in our bag? Who cleans the store?"
3. Plan with children for a follow-up trip to make clearer observations on roles of store personnel.
4. Plan with children for creative dramatization of store play, following Lang. 4.90.

Further Reference

Language 4.90

Appendix

Appendix

CHILD BEHAVIOR TEST (CBT)

Name _____ Previous School _____

Birthdate _____ Age as of 9/1/71_____ yrs_____ months Date enrolled _____

Code: M=Mastery   + = Partial Mastery   0 = Nonmastery

Item	Date			Item	Date		
SOCIOLOGY AND LANGUAGE				GEOGRAPHY			
1. Names				**7. Positional Terms**			
1.1 self				7.1 on			
1.2 another				7.2 under			
1.3 teacher				7.3 in front of			
1.4 aide				7.4 between			
2. Name Recognition				**8. Spatial Positions**			
2.1 first name				8.1 top left			
2.2 last name				8.2 bottom right			
2.3 full name				8.3 middle			
3. Name Writing				8.4 top middle			
3.1 first name				COGNITIVE SKILLS AND MATHEMATICS			
3.2 full name				**9. Patterns**			
4. Color Identification				9.1 R-B-R-B-R-B			
4.1 blue				9.2 RR-BB-RR-BB			
4.2 gray				9.3 BB-R-BB-R			
4.3 pink				9.4 pencil-block-pencil-block			
4.4 white				9.5 RR-BB-R B			
4.5 orange				**10. Quantity Comparison**			
4.6 yellow				10.1 selects: more than			
4.7 red & brown				10.2 less than			
4.8 green & black				10.3 creates: more than			
5. Alphabet				10.4 less than			
5.1 upper case				**11. Counting Objects**			
5.2 lower case				11.1 1-5			
6. Reading				11.2 6-10			
6.1 Cat sat				11.3 11-15			
6.2 Fat cat sat							
6.3 Is the cat fat?							
6.4 The fat cat has a hat							

Item	Date			Item	Date		
12. Numerals				13.6 10c (another way)			
12.1 copies: 1-3							
12.2 4-6				14. Same-Different			
12.3 7-9				14.1 same object			
12.4 writes on				14.2 same color			
recall: 1-3				14.3 same shape			
12.5 4-6				14.4 different object			
12.6 7-9				14.5 different color			
				14.6 different shape			
13. Money							
13.1 identifies: nickel				15. Color-Form Sort			
13.2 dime				15.1 color			
13.3 quarter				15.2 form			
13.4 penny							
13.5 selects equivalents: 10c							

INSTRUCTIONS FOR DIAGNOSTIC TEST BATTERY-CBT

Top of Sheet

Enter name of child, last name first. If child is known to have had previous school experience, enter brief note, such as "Summer Head Start," "Full Year Head Start," "Day Care-2 years," "Nursery School-1 year" or similar notes. Enter date child was enrolled in class.

1. Name Identification — Possible Codes

 1.1 "What is your name"?   M   0
 1.2 "What is the name of another child in your class"?
   (Accept the first name only)   M   0
 1.3 "What is the name of your teacher"?   M   0
 1.4 "What is the name of_____"?   M   0
   (Use the common term for the teacher's helper, such as Aide, Assistant, or the like)

2. Name Recognition

 2.1 (Show the child a list of 4 first names, written in manuscript, one of which is his first name, the others the first names of other members of the class)
   "Which is your name"?   M   0
 2.2 (Repeat 2.1 using 4 last names)   M   0
 2.3 (Repeat 2.1, using 4 full names)   M   0

3. Name Writing

 (Give the child a clean piece of paper and a crayon)
 3.1 "Write your name."   M   +   0
   (If he writes only one name-first or last)
 3.2 "Write your other name too."   M   +   0
 (Score √ for mastery only if all letters are written recognizably.)

4. Color Identification

 Place 10 skeins of yarn in front of the child: gray, pink, red, green, black, orange, white, yellow blue, brown.
 Each time the child gives you a skein in response to your questions, replace it in the pile in front of him.
 4.1 "Give me the blue one."   M   0
 4.2 "Give me the gray one."   M   0
 4.3 "Give me the pink one."   M   0
 4.4 "Give me the white one."   M   0
 4.5 "Give me the orange one."   M   0
 4.6 "Give me the yellow one."   M   0
 4.7 "Give me the red one and the brown one."   M   0
 4.8 "Give me the green one and the black one."   M   0

5. Alphabet Letters

    Use flannel letters, magnetic letters or any other precut
    letters. If you have none, write letters on separate cards.
    5.1 Place an assortment of 15 upper case alphabet let-
         ters in front of child. Ask child to select letter as
         you name it. Return letter to assortment before
         requesting another letter. Score +, for partial mas-
         tery, if child selects at least 8 letters correctly. Re-
         peat procedure, until all letters are used.   M   +   0
    5.2 Repeat procedure, using lower-case letters.   M   +   0
    If desired, enter on back of sheet letters child has not
    identified.

6. Reading

    Show the child the four reading cards one at a time and
    ask him to read each in turn. Each sentence, written in
    manuscript, should be on a separate card.

    6.1 Cat sat   M   +   0
    6.2 Fat cat sat   M   +   0
    6.3 Is the cat fat?   M   +   0
    6.4 The fat cat has a hat   M   +   0

7. Positional Terms

    Place a block and 2 miniature trucks in front of the child.
    7.1 "Put the block on the truck."   M   +   0
    7.2 "Put the block under the truck."   M   +   0
    7.3 "Put the block in front of the truck."   M   +   0
    7.4 "Put the block between the 2 trucks."   M   +   0

8. Spatial Positions

    Present the child with a sheet of paper and five small
    blocks.
    8.1 "Put a block on top of the page in the left hand
         corner."   M   +   0
    8.2 "Put a block on the bottom of the page in the right
         corner."   M   +   0
    8.3 "Put a block in the middle of the page."   M   +   0
    8.4 "Put a block in the middle of the top of the page." M   +   0

9. Patterns

Give child 5 red and 5 blue counting cubes. Make the
following patterns, one at a time, and ask child to "Make
a row just like mine."

9.1	R-B-R-B-R-B	M	0
9.2	RR-BB-RR-BB	M	0
9.3	BB-R-BB-R	M	0

Give child 2 pencils and 2 blocks. Make a pencil-block
pattern.

9.4	Ask child to "Finish the row."	M	0

Make following incomplete pattern: RR-BB-R   -   B.

9.5	Ask child to "Put the missing items in the pattern."	M	0

10. Quantity Comparison

Use 20 tongue depressors or popsicle sticks.

10.1	Place 5 in a row in front of teacher. Put sets of different sizes in random order in front of child. "Which has more, yours or mine"? Repeat 4 times, varying number placed before child	M	+	0
10.2	Repeat 10.1, except "Which has less, yours or mine?"	M	+	0
10.3	Place 5 in a row in front of teacher. Hand child 15 sticks. "Make a set which has more than mine."	M		0
10.4	Repeat 10.3, except "Make a set which has less than mine."	M		0

11. Counting

Place the following sets of crayons in front of child, one
set at a time.
"How many crayons are here"?

11.1	5 crayons, 3 crayons, 4 crayons	M	+	0
11.2	7 crayons, 10 crayons, 9 crayons	M	+	0
11.3	12 crayons, 14 crayons, 15 crayons	M	+	0

12. Numerals

Give child paper and pencil or crayon.

12.1	Show child numerals 1, 2, 3 and ask him to copy them.	M	+	0
12.2	Repeat for numerals 4 to 6.	M	+	0
12.3	Repeat for numerals 7 to 9.	M	+	0

If desired, enter on back of sheet numerals child does not
copy or write.

12.4	Give child a fresh piece of paper and ask him to write the numbers as you call out 1 to 9 in random order. Do not show him any to copy.	M	+	0

13. Coin Identification

Present the child with the following coins in random fashion: 3 nickels, 2 dimes, 1 quarter.

13.1	Hold up the nickel. "What is this?"	M	0
13.2	Repeat with a quarter.	M	0
13.3	Repeat with a penny.	M	0
13.4	Repeat with a dime.	M	0
13.5	"If I buy something for 10 cents, show me how I can pay for it with these coins."	M	0
13.6	"Now, show me another way I can pay for it."	M	0

14. Same-Different

Present the child with 2 identical sets of 6 common objects, as follows:

        2 white plastic spoons
        2 white plastic forks
        2 blue counting cubes
        2 blue wooden beads
        2 yellow wooden triangles
        2 yellow wooden circles

14.1	Pick up one of each pair of objects, in turn. "Please pick up an object which is the same as this."	M	0
14.2	Repeat the procedure in 14.1, "Please pick up an object which is the same color as this."	M	0
14.3	Repeat the procedure in 14.1, "Please pick up an object which is the same shape as this."	M	0
14.4	Repeat the procedure in 14.1. "Please pick up an object which is different from this one."	M	0
14.5	Repeat the procedure in 14.1. "Please pick up something with a different color."	M	0
14.6	Repeat the procedure in 14.1. "Please pick up something with a different shape."	M	0

15. Classification of Objects

Present the child with the following in random order:
        2 white squares
        2 white circles

2 white triangles
1 blue square
1 blue circle
1 blue triangle

Use wooden, plastic or construction paper objects. Any other 2 distinctly different colors may be substituted for white and blue.

15.1 "Here are 2 boxes. Put together in each box the things that go together." Code for mastery if child sorts by color.	M	0
15.2 Present same objects in random order again with 3 boxes." Here are 3 boxes. Put together in each box the things that go together."	M	0

Code √ for mastery if child sorts by shape.

RECOMMENDED PROGRAM SEQUENCE: FIRST MONTH

Activity and Approximate Time[1]	Teacher Role	Guidelines for Teaching
Work Period - 9 A.M.	Centers of Interest: 3 to 5 centers 1. Housekeeping area, limited number of props. 2. Block area with selected accessories. 3. Easel with 4 colors of paint. 4. Manipulative materials, such as pegs and pegboard, colored cubes, tinkertoys, math materials. Teacher Role: 1. Greet children individually. 2. Engage children directly in play. 3. Talk to children conversationally.	Uncluttered setting with clearly defined spaces for play and storage of materials and equipment. Attractive arrangement and attractive materials communicating clear range of choices.
Clean-up - 9:40 A.M.	Advise children individually of impending change of activity. "It is playtime now. Soon, it will be time to clean up so we can have some juice and crackers." Initiate clean-up by helping small groups of children to complete routine. Where possible, arrange an easy flow into bathroom and wash-up as each child completes his part of the clean-up tasks	Respect for uniqueness of each child, including tolerance for range of maturity and pacing. Demonstration with verbalization and *repetition* of demonstration. Positive reinforcement, praise.
Snack - 10:00 A.M.	Snack in small groups with one adult participating with each group. Engage children in conversation, as "Tell me about your family," and in recall of play period activities.	Demonstration with verbalization.
Music - 10:20 A.M.	Lead group action games and simple songs.	Appealing to children's interests. Accepting participation by observation.
Story - 10:40 A.M.	Small story groups. Simple stories told or read.	If no more than one adult is available, omit this period and offer small group stories during playtime.
Discussion - 10:50 A.M.	Lead group discussion recalling events of the day and anticipating the next school day.	
Departure - 11:00 A.M.	Greet children's escorts and offer personal goodbye to each child.	

[1] Adjust time to schedule for arrival and departure time

TEACHING PLANS: FIRST MONTH

Behavioral Goals	Teaching Strategies

SOCIOLOGY

Self-Knowing

Children respond to and produce own full names.

Children produce names of others in class, adults and children.
Children recognize their own written name.

Children recognize their own image on a photograph.

Self-Valuing

Children select own activities.

Group Membership

Family: Children name family members and their relationship.

Children identify some attributes of family membership. Also Language: Children talk spontaneously as they work and play.

Class: Children recapitulate and anticipate the classroom schedule of events.

Language: Children talk spontaneously.

Children narrate class experiences and produce language freely for tape recording.

Children recognize their own voices on recorded tape and contribute to and comply with classroom rules

Mathematics: Children sort objects into subsets. See Math, 5.11.

Cognitive Skills: Children put like things together. See Cog. Skills 2.10.

1. Offer personal greetings to each child and his escort on arrival and departure, using full names. Introduce self and aide.
2. Give each child prepared nametag, necklace-type, coded for child's identification by color or decal, same as used on child's cubbie. As children become familiar with routine, ask them to find their own tag. Help as needed.
3. Use full names of children in some activities, such as at snack time. Distribute cookies saying, "This cookie is for John Jones. This cookie is for Susie Brown."
4. As children become accustomed to routine of using full names, introduce playfulness by making errors and asking children to help correct your errors.
5. Use first names liberally.
6. Introduce name chart with attendance-taking procedure, using photograph or decal.
7. Feature free choice of materials, equipment, activity and playmates during activity period.
8. At snack time, children are arranged in small groups, and conversation started about members of families. Encourage each child to name his family members and their relationship to him, as *brother, sister*. In subsequent discussions, elicit more detail as to the family member's roles and responsibilities, such as, "Mother cooks. I dress myself. My sister dresses the baby." See Lang. 4.10.
9. Emphasize the sequence of activities in class as, "Now it's time to play." Then, "Soon it will be time to put things away."
10. Just before going home, lead a brief group discussion, listing the sequence of the day's activities and anticipating next day's sequence. Elicit increasing detail from children over time. Use tape recorder to record children's descriptions of play activities, and to check group's prediction of next day's program. See Soc. 7.10, Lang. 4.10, and 4.11.
11. In each center of interest begin to establish the "ground rules" for use of materials by demonstrating and verbalizing, and using positive reinforcement, such as praise.
12. At clean-up time, demonstrate and verbalize the pattern for stroage of materials in boxes and on shelves. For example, "All the pegs go in this box. All the colored cubes go in this box." See Math, 5.11. Cog. Skills 2.10.

GEOGRAPHY

Children identify and locate key locations and pathways inside the school building.

Sociology—Group membership: Children find the way to their classrooms and other key locations in the school.

Language: Children narrate class experiences and produce language freely for tape recording. Children recognize their own voices on recorded tape.

1. Take children on walk inside school building identifying and labelling important locations and pathways, such as main office and auditorium. See Geog. 8.30.
2. Repeat walks inside school building labelling additional rooms and eliciting increasing detail of observation. See Geog. 8.30.
3. Ask children to recapitulate walk and tape recorder discussion. Offer opportunity to listen to tape soon after recording and encourage repetitive listening. See Lang. 4.11.

MUSIC

Children sing new and familiar songs.

Sociology—Self-knowing: Children recognize a description of their clothing.

Language: Children use precise name labels and descriptive terms.

Children jump to the rhythm of their name.

Children produce appropriate movements to words of song and match other children's movements.

Cognitive Skills: Children copy "same" motions and make different" motions upon request.

1. Find out which songs children know and sing them daily. See Music 3.10, 3.11.
2. Gradually, add new songs and chants featuring ones that include names of children such as, "Mary wore a red dress." See Music 3.10, 3.11.
3. Introduce Jump to Your Name game. See Music 3.20.
4. Later, introduce action-song game that requires imitative behavior, such as, "Did you ever see a lassie." See Music 3.30, Cog. Skills 2.00.

SCIENCE

Children identify observable properties of objects and label them.

Children identify and label changes in food materials.

Language: Children use precise name labels and descriptive terms.

Children identify and label changes in materials as evidence of interaction. Children use hindsight to compare materials after interaction. Also: Mathematics: Children match a set of objects to a given set.

1. Make playdough with children. See Sci. 6.21, Math. 5.10, Lang. 4.10.
2. Help children mix fruit juice from frozen concentrate. See Sci. 6.20.
3. Invite children to make a collage of hand objects or craft objects. See Sci. 6.10.

MATHEMATICS

Children pair off as partners

Children match one object to one person.

Children differentiate members of sets from nonmembers of sets.

Children sort sets into subsets.

Language: Children use precise name labels and descriptive terms.

1. Help children pick partners for such activities as music games and taking a walk. See Math. 5.10.
2. At snack time, ask a child to distribute napkins, cups, cookies, matching one object to one child. At music time, ask a child to distribute musical instruments. See Math. 5.10.
3. Introduce Pick-Up game with magnet and set of objects. See Math. 5.11.
4. At clean-up time, demonstrate and verbalize the pattern for storage of materials in boxes and on shelves. For example, "All the short blocks on this top shelf. All the long blocks go on this bottom shelf. "See Math, 5.11, Lang. 4.10.

COGNITIVE SKILLS

Children use miniature objects to copy a pattern of miniature objects.

Language: Children use precise name labels, descriptive terms, and positional terms.

1. Invite one child at a time to work with you playing a copying game with the objects. Keep episodes brief and try to work with each child *at least* once a week after the first week. See Cog. Skills 2.20.

LANGUAGE

Children talk spontaneously as they work and play.

Children use precise labels and descriptive terms.

Children enjoy hearing stories read.

1. Participate in discussions with children at snack time and other times when the discussion does not intrude on children's play. See Lang. 4.10.
2. Use precise language liberally in all activities in which you are participating with children.
   Cognitive Skills 2.10, 2.20.
   Music 3.10, 3.11, 3.20, 3.30
   Language 4.10, 4.101, Math 5.10, 5.11
   Science 6.10, 6.20, 6.21
   Sociology 7.10, 7.11
   Geography 8.30
3. Read stories daily to small groups of interested children. See Lang. 4.101.

RECOMMENDED CHANGES IN PROGRAM SEQUENCES
FOR SECOND MONTH OF PROGRAM [1]

Music—9:00 A.M. (Initiate before work period)

Initiate musical activities with total group, such as songs and tone matching, movement to music, Jump to Your Name game, or use of rhythm instruments.

Work Period—9:20 A.M.

1. Offer free choice of selected activities, such as: block play, easel painting, housekeeping play, manipulative materials.
2. Initiate tutorial sequences with individual children, while most children are engaged in self-selected work and play activities.

Use this opening activity to address children by name in songs or chants.

Pace the music briskly and feature fun and movement. Include variety in musical activities. Lengthen or shorten the music period, according to children's skill in total group activity and their involvement at the time. Release individual children to wish to engage in other activities.

Convey rules for use of materials by demonstration and verbalization.

Help children become engaged in self-selected activities, if necessary, by suggestion, and guidance of specific children.

Arrange clear work centers, with needed materials readily available.

Help children learn how to take care of emergencies such as using newspaper and sponges to wipe up spilled paint.

As behavior problems occur, handle them by repeating classroom rules. Redirecting children or assigning one teacher to work with child who needs detailed supervision.

Invite a child to tackle a task specified in the instructional samples. Let other children watch, if they like, and engage them in similar tasks, as time and materials permit.

Be flexible in use of your time, while children's ability to stay with tasks or to play with minimal adult supervision grows and becomes more dependable.

Self-Service Snack—10:00 A.M.

Continue work period.

Continue tape recorder, and small group game, such as lotto.

Continue tutorial sequences with individual children.

Alert children to impending 10:50 clean-up time.

Guide helper tasks, in setting up snack items.

Arrange snack in uncluttered space.

Give children as much responsibility as they can handle in pouring juice or opening milk cartons and disposing of used items.

Announce availability of snack quietly and individually or give this task to a child.

Help children to manage self-service snacks without interrupting other activities which may continue during this period.

[1] Adjust time to schedule for arrival, lunch and departure times.

Clean-up—11:00 A.M.

Initiate clean up.

Help wherever needed, giving children major responsibility of cleaning and putting away.

Continue to help children clean up and put away materials.

Include some regular helper tasks in the clean-up routines, such as:

1. Fill a wastepaper basket with litter from floor;
2. Sponge tables;
3. Check puzzles for completeness;
4. Wash paint brushes;
5. Arrange book corner attractively.

Sing and chant about the clean-up activities, and use music as a filler until all children are finished.

Group Evaluation—11:15 A.M.

Help children recapitulate day's program sequence and anticipate next day's program.

Ask questions and summarize briefly.

Dress for Dismissal—11:25 A.M.

Announce time to get dressed.

Arrange clear, efficient routines for finding clothes and dressing. Encourage self-help and mutual helpfulness. Demonstrate and collaborate with children to encourage independence in buttoning, zipping, and sequence of dressing activities.

Dismissal—11:30 A.M.

Dismiss children with humor and affection, individually.

Work with parents to develop good dismissal routines, so that classroom work is not interrupted and the maximum time is available for children's school learning.

SAMPLE WEEKLY TEACHING PLAN

Week #7

Behavioral Goals	Initiate	Continue
Cognitive Skills 2.00		
1. Children use colored objects to copy a pattern of colored objects.	1. New patterns, as in Item 6, Cog. Skills 2.22, in the sequence suggested on Chart A. Cog. Skills 2.21.	Patterning with concrete objects, and color patterns, as outlined in Chart A, Cog. Skills 2.21.
2. Children match picture to object labeling them as the same.	2. Slap-Jack Game, Cog. Skills 2.12, to match picture to objects.	Use of object boxes, combining objects that are the same, as in Cog. Skills 2.10 and 2.11.
Music 3.00		
3. Children match tones, call them *same*.	3. Match *same* singing and xylophone tones, as in Music 3.40.	Singing, chants, songs with movement Jump to Your Name game, as in Music 3.10 to 3.12, 3.20, 3.30.
Language 4.00		
4. Children narrate class experiences.	4. Construct a story booklet about a cooking experience, as in Lang. 4.64. See Item 6, Science, below.	Eliciting and extending language in play, story, listening, tape recording, lotto game, name replication, as in Lang. 4.10 to 4.12, 4.20.
Mathematics 5.00		
5. Children compare 2 unequal sets of objects	5. Happy Clown game, as in Math. 5.30.	Geometric shapes, one-to-one matching, members of sets and subsets, copying model sets, as in Math. 5.10 to 5.12, 5.20.
Science 6.0		
6a. Children identify observable properties of objects.	6. Cooking experience, such as orange icing for Halloween cookies, as in Sci. 6.20. Use this experience for content of booklet suggested in Language, above.	Playdough and soap bubbles.

Craft activities to identify properties of objects. |
| 6b. Children identify and label changes in properties of objects. | | Experimenting with magnets and water to identify properties of objects, as in Sci. 7.10, 6.11, 6.20, 6.21. |
| **Sociology** | | |
| 7a. Children participate in craft activities related to holiday celebrations. | 7. Halloween Masks and Jack O' Lantern, as in Items 2 and 3 of Chart A, Soc. 7.20 | Recalling sequence of day's activities.

Attendance-taking with name chart.

Craft projects, such as collages, mobiles |
| 7b. Children take pride in their products. | | Art activities with paint, crayon, clay. As in Soc. 7.10, 7.20, 7.21, and 7.30. |

Appendix

Geography

8. Children use physical objects to represent physical space.

8. Strip of paper represents streets in block building, as in Geog. 8.40

Economics

9. Children use money to make a purchase.

9. Trip to buy a pumpkin, as in Econ. 9.10.

Obstacle Game

Walk inside school and in neighborhood, as in Geog. 8.10, 8.30, and 8.31.

ACTIVITIES ANALYSIS FORM (AAF)

Use of Form

1. Read definitions of categories, on pages 235 to 238.
2. Use a stopwatch to obtain samples of teaching behavior on a time-sampling basis, following one of these alternatives:
   a. Code teacher behavior for the first full minute in each five-minute interval, for three consecutive periods. Repeat this procedure, after a ten-minute break.
   b. Code teacher behavior for the first minute in each three-minute interval for three consecutive periods. Repeat procedure for each program activity, such as, "work-period," "clean-up," "snack," and "outdoor play."
3. To code teacher behavior, number each teacher move as it occurs in sequence, for each minute observation period, numbering in the vertical column for that period. Or use a check or tally mark, instead of a number, eliminating the sequence in which each move occurs. Numbering teacher moves in sequence makes it possible to analyze repeated patterns of moves. Tallying moves without noting the sequence in which they occur simply provides a distribution of the types of moves teachers make.
4. It is possible to videotape teaching samples and code the teacher's behavior on replay, using any time-sampling desired.
5. Since this instrument is offered as a tool for self-analysis and judgments about needed changes in teaching behavior, it is suggested for use by pairs of teachers or students who are interested in mutual support for self-study and judgments about their teaching skills and styles.

ACTIVITY ANALYSIS FORM (AAF)

Definition of Categories

I. Instructional Moves

   1. Nonintervention: Teacher is in immediate proximity of an ongoing activity. She is not involved in any form of teacher move, apparently watching.
      a. Teacher sits next to child working with manipulative materials; watches, sits, but does not converse with child or become actively involved with materials.
      b. Group game (music or other) is in process and being led by a child. Teacher is with group as a nonparticipant either verbally or actively.
   2. Collaboration: Teacher and child work together on the same project. Teacher may direct and control the cooperative activity or she may encourage and assist. Teacher is always an active participant with child.
      a. Teacher and children are reciting nursery rhymes or chants.
      b. Teacher and child are working together on a woodwork construction.

Teacher assists child.

3. Demonstration: Teacher shows an example of an object, action and/or procedure. Or teacher illustrates the meaning of a verbal utterance.

4. Giving information: Teacher offers facts, explanations, descriptions either verbally or non-verbally.
   a. Teacher tells children the name of the day of the week.
   b. In response to an inquiry from child about where are scissors, teacher points to a shelf without any verbal utterance.

5. Giving directions: Teacher directs children's action in an instructional context or teacher makes a statement that is a directive to action.
   Ex: "Put that chair under the table."

6. Affective-involvement stimulation: Teacher encourages and/or praises child relative to his on-going activity or products of his activity:
   a. "That's a beautiful building you're making Johnny"!
   b. "What lovely colors you are using, Susie"!
   c. "Very nice," "good," etc.

7. Cognitive stimulation—feedback: Teacher remarks on children's activities or products that serve to give verbal labels or cognitive stimulation (clarify, compare, etc.):
   a. "Oh Johnny, you are using orange and red and blue paint."
   b. "Look, those two colors, blue and yellow, are mixing to make green."
   c. "I see this building is higher than that one."

8. Cognitive stimulation—testing: Teacher questions child as to the content, processes, labels of the materials and products of his work or of stimuli she is introducing.
   a. Child brings painting to teacher. She questions and points, "What color is this?"
   b. Teacher comments to block building, "How many blocks do you have?" or "Where is the roof on this house?" (if roof is evident). If roof were not evident, it would reflect the cognitive stimulation of extending activity.
   c. Teacher shows a triangle to children and asks, "Who knows what this is?"

9. Cognitive stimulation—extending: Teacher comments or questions to child redirect his energies back to the activity to extend it. Can also apply to stimulus for extending verbal utterances.
   "Is this block construction large enough to be a house for the family?"

10. Reading, writing and recitation: Teacher reads story, poem or other written matter. Teacher writes in manuscript as children observe. Teacher recites a poem or familiar story.

11. Operating equipment: Teacher operates tape recorder, projector, victrola, etc.

12. Other (specify):

II. Behavioral Moves: Dealing with children's feelings or behavior

13. Dealing with feelings-positive: Teacher comments, remarks, utterances, actions serve to aid child's feeling of acceptance, belonging, adequacy: not specifically directed to change in behavior.
   a. Teacher comments upon dress or grooming of child, "What a pretty

dress you're wearing!"

    b. Teacher acceptance of individual feelings, preferences, attitudes, such as, "You look sad today."

    c. Teacher approval through remarks "that's nice," smiles, or physical affection.

    d. Pats on shoulder, holding hands, etc.

14. Dealing with feelings—negative: Teacher rejection of individual expressions, preferences, attitudes without identifiable instructional act: distinguished from controlling behavior by lack of immediate social behavioral referent.

    a. Child: "I don't like my mommy today."
        Teacher: "That's not nice. All children love their mommies."

    b. Child looks sad, but is not overtly crying.
        Teacher: "Don't be a crybaby." If child were crying and teacher responded in this manner, it would reflect controlling behavior-negative.

    c. "Some children in this class were naughty today. I don't like naughty children."

15. Controlling Behavior—positive: Teacher guidance of child in a social relationship that aids in development of self-control, or provides alternative patterns of problem resolution: guidance projects the quality of an emotionally supportive relationship as against a rejecting, punitive relationship; includes physical controls, verbal guidance and limit setting behavior directed toward helping child function more adequately within the group structure. Can include punishments, without overt rejection either by voice, tone, words or actions. For example, teacher may hold a child firmly, restraining his actions, while saying in a friendly tone, "I won't let you hurt Jimmy."

16. Controlling Behavior—negative: Teacher attempts control of child behavior through threatening, punitive and rejecting responses: judgmental, reflecting harsh, rejective manner by tone of voice or verbalization.

    a. Teacher: "Johnny, stop that! You're a naughty boy!"

    b. Teacher: "Johnny, get away. You're just a nuisance."

    c. Teacher: "Why aren't you a good boy, like Johnny?"

III. Management Moves: Classroom management

17. Arrangements (Children): Teacher direction of routines, eating, toileting, dressing, clean-up with no identifiable instructional move.
    Ex: "Get on line"; "put toys away now"; "throw napkins away"; etc.

18. Teacher activity—housekeeping: General auxiliary clean-up not specifically related to a child or group of children.

    a. pushing chairs under the table, picking up materials, equipment, etc.

19. Teacher activity—school personnel: Interaction with classroom personnel, or other school personnel, verbal or nonverbal.

20. Teacher activity—family members: Interaction with members of children's families.

21. Other (specify)

IV. Uninvolved Behavior

22. Not involved: Personal grooming, reading newspaper, looking out window, and so forth.

ACTIVITY ANALYSIS FORM
(AAF)

Date: _____   Attendance: _____

School: _____   Recorder: _____

Teacher: _____   _____

Clock Time _____

Program Context _____

Group Context _____

I. Instructional Moves

1. Nonintervention
2. Collaboration
3. Demonstration
4. Giving information
5. Giving directions
6. Affective-involvement stimulation
7. Cognitive stimulation: feedback
8. Cognitive stimulation: testing
9. Cognitive stimulation: extending
10. Reading, writing, and recitation
11. Operating equipment
12. Other (specify)

II. Behavioral Moves

13. Dealing with feelings: positive
14. Dealing with feelings: negative
15. Controlling behavior: positive
16. Controlling behavior: negative

Instructions
and
Horizontal Codes
(Use Stopwatch)

Program Context Code

1. Free play
2. Routines
3. Outdoor play
4. Transition
5. Story period
6. Structured activity
    a. physical
    b. physical-verbal
    c. physical-manpulative
    d   verbal
    e. verbal manipulative
    f. manipulative
    g. physical-verbal-manipulative

Group Context

A. Teacher—total group
B. Teacher—small group
C. Teacher—individual child
D. Child—small group
E. Child-total group
F. Child—individual child
G. Teacher alone

III. Management Moves

    17. Arrangements (children)

    18. Teacher activity: house-keeping

    19. Teacher activity: school personnel

    20. Teacher activity: family members

    21. Other (specify)

IV. Uninvolved Behavior

    22. Not involved

CHILD PROGRESS FORM

Mastery Code

1 = mastery
2 = progress
3 = nonmastery
4 = no interest

Name _____

Birthdate _____

Date Enrolled _____

Content Area: Cognitive Skills

Card No.	Date	MC*	Date	MC	Date	MC	Date	MC	Date	MC	Comments
2.10											
2.11											
2.12											
2.13											
2.20											
2.21											
2.22											
2.23											
2.24											
2.25											
2.30											

*Mastery Code

CHILD PROGRESS FORM

Mastery Code

1 = mastery
2 = progress
3 = nonmastery
4 = no interest

Name _____

Birthdate _____

Date Enrolled _____

Content Area: Music

Card No.	Date	MC*	Date	MC	Date	MC	Date	MC	Date	MC	Comments
3.10											
3.11											
3.12											
3.20											
3.21											
3.30											
3.31											
3.32											
3.33											
3.34											
3.40											
3.41											
3.42											
3.43											
3.50											
3.51											

*Mastery Code

CHILD PROGRESS FORM

Mastery Code

1 = mastery
2 = progress
3 = nonmastery
4 = no interest

Name _____

Birthdate _____

Date Enrolled _____

Content Area: Language

Card No.	Date	MC*	Date	MC	Date	MC	Date	MC	Date	MC	Comments
4.10											
4.101											
4.11											
4.12											
4.13											
4.14											
4.15											
4.16											
4.17											
4.18											
4.19											
4.20											
4.21											
4.22											
4.50											
4.60											
4.61											
4.62											
4.621											
4.63											
4.64											
4.80											
4.90											

*Mastery Code

CHILD PROGRESS FORM

Mastery Code

1 = mastery
2 = progress
3 = nonmastery
4 = no interest

Name _____

Birthdate_____

Date Enrolled _____

Content Area: Mathematics

Card No.	Date	MC*	Date	MC	Date	MC	Date	MC	Date	MC	Comments
5.10											
5.11											
5.12											
5.13											
5.20											
5.30											
5.31											
5.32											
5.42											
5.44											
5.45											
5.50											
5.51											
5.52											
5.53											
5.60											
5.70											
5.71											
5.72											
5.80											
5.81											
5.82											
5.90											

*Mastery Code

CHILD PROGRESS FORM

Mastery Code

1 = mastery
2 = progress
3 = nonmastery
4 = no interest

Name _____

Birthdate _____

Date Enrolled _____

Content Area: Science

Card No.	Date	MC*	Date	MC	Date	MC	Date	MC	Date	MC	Comments
6.10											
6.11											
6.20											
6.21											
6.22											
6.23											
6.30											
6.40											

* Mastery Code

CHILD PROGRESS FORM

Mastery Code

1 = mastery
2 = progress
3 = nonmastery
4 = no interest

Name _____

Birthdate _____

Date Enrolled _____

Content Area: Sociology

Card No.	Date	MC*	Date	MC	Date	MC	Date	MC	Date	MC	Comments
7.10											
7.11											
7.12											
7.13											
7.14											
7.20											
7.21											
7.22											
7.30											

*Mastery Code

Appendix

CHILD PROGRESS FORM

Mastery Code

1 = mastery
2 = progress
3 = nonmastery
4 = no interest

Name _____

Birthdate _____

Date Enrolled _____

Content Area: Geography

Card No.	Date	MC*	Date	MC	Date	MC	Date	MC	Date	MC	Comments
8.10											
8.20											
8.30											
8.31											
8.32											
8.40											
8.41											

CHILD PROGRESS FORM

Mastery Code

1 = mastery
2 = progress
3 = nonmastery
4 = no interest

Name _____

Birthdate _____

Date Enrolled _____

Content Area: Economics

Card No.	Date	MC*	Date	MC	Date	MC	Date	MC	Date	MC	Comments
9.10											
9.11											
9.12											
9.13											
9.14											

*Mastery Code